Explode The Code®

Teacher's Guide for Books 3 and 4

Nancy Hall

School Specialty, Inc.

Cambridge and Toronto

Acquisitions/Development: Sethany Rancier Alongi
Editor: Elissa Gershowitz
Cover Design: David Parra
Typesetting: Kathleen Richards
Managing Editor: Sheila Neylon

Printed in Benton Harbor, MI, in March 2012
ISBN 978-0-8388-0854-2

8 9 PPG 12

Introduction

The No Child Left Behind Act of 2001 mandates that states formulate reading standards for each grade with the goal of having all children reading proficiently by the end of third grade. Federal money, through Reading First funds, will be available to help achieve these goals for states adopting reading programs in which the early reading skills of phonemic awareness, phonics, fluency, vocabulary, and comprehension are systematically and explicitly taught. *Explode The Code®* meets these standards.

Systematic, Direct Teaching of Phonics

Jeanne Chall's *Learning to Read: The Great Debate*—an extensive review of classroom, laboratory, and clinical research—revealed the efficacy of a direct, explicit, systematic teaching of decoding skills. Chall concluded that code emphasis programs produced better results, "not only in terms of the mechanical aspects of literacy alone, as was once supposed, but also in terms of the ultimate goals of reading instruction—comprehension and possibly even speed of reading" (Chall 1967, 307).

Even as new understandings about learning and teaching have evolved in the years since 1967, these findings have been repeatedly reconfirmed (Bond and Dykstra 1967; Chall 1983; Adams 1990; National Reading Panel 2000). In 2000, the National Reading Panel presented its findings of studies comparing phonics instruction with other kinds of instruction, published since 1970. Focusing on kindergarten through sixth grade, the panel concluded that systematic phonics instruction enhanced children's ability to read, spell, and comprehend text, particularly in the younger grades. These results were especially evident in the word-reading skills of disabled readers and low socioeconomic children, and for the spelling skills of good readers.

Chall and Popp write of "two kinds of meaning—meaning of the medium (the print) and the meaning of the message (the ideas)" (1996, 2). Knowledge of phonics gives students the ability to decode print, which in turn reveals the message ideas. The more words early readers can recognize, the more accessible meaning becomes. Children who have difficulty identifying words lack the fluency needed to concentrate on meaning (Rasinsky 2000). Conversely, children who are given direct, systematic instruction in decoding skills have the tools for developing fluent, meaningful reading. Furthermore, they have the tools to produce print and consequently express their thoughts in writing, which in turn reinforces their word identification skills (Ehri 1998).

Explode The Code offers a complete systematic phonics program for the elementary grades. Phonetic elements and patterns, carefully sequenced to consider both frequency of use and difficulty, are presented in sequence and practiced in a series of instructive workbooks. Teacher's Guides and Keys accompany all the books.

The first three books in the *Explode The Code* series—Books A, B, and C—focus on visual identification of consonants, their written lowercase letter forms, and their sound–symbol relationships. An engaging, colorful wall chart with felt objects representing key words for the twenty-six letters of the alphabet may be used to introduce children to the names and sounds of the lowercase letters and/or to reinforce lessons in books A, B, and C. An activity book with instructions for thirty-five games comes with the wall chart. Key word picture–letter cards are also provided.

The remaining eight books—*Explode The Code* Books 1–8—progress through the vowel sounds and patterns, consonant clusters and digraphs, syllables, and suffixes. Posttests are found at the end of each workbook. If extra practice is needed, an additional workbook for reinforcement accompanies each of books 1–6. Code Cards reinforce and review the letter sounds taught in *Explode The Code* Books 1–3½.

Through systematic direct teaching of phonics using *Explode The Code,* the following successes in reading and writing occur:

- The alphabetic principle is firmly established.
- Phonological awareness skills are fostered alongside the phonics teaching.
- Understanding of how sound–symbol relationships permit words and text to be decoded and encoded is fully developed and practiced, enhancing fluency and automaticity.
- Students of varying language and skill needs are accommodated through vocabulary and concept building, exposure to differing approaches to teaching phonics, and flexible grouping and use of the materials.
- See more about the research for this series at http://www.epsbooks.com.

References

Adams, M. J. (1990). *Beginning to Read: Thinking and Learning about Print.* Cambridge, MA: MIT Press.

Bond, G. & Dykstra, R. (1967). "The cooperative research program in first grade reading." *Reading Research Quarterly* 2:5-142.

Chall, J. S. (1967, 1983). *Learning to Read: The Great Debate.* New York: McGraw Hill.

Chall, J. S. & Popp, H. M. (1996). *Teaching and Assessing Phonics, Why, What, When, How: A Guide for Teachers.* Cambridge, MA: Educators Publishing Service.

Ehri, L. C. (1998). "Grapheme-phoneme knowledge is essential for learning to read words in English." In: Metsala, J. L. & Ehri, L. C. (eds.) *Word Recognition in Beginning Literacy.* Mahwah, NJ: Erlbaum, 3-40.

National Reading Panel (2000). *Teaching Children to Read: An Evidence Based Assessment of the Scientific Research Literature on Reading and its Implication for Reading Instruction: Reports of the Subgroups.* Washington: National Institute of Child Health and Development.

Rasinsky, T. V. (2000). "Does speed matter in reading?" *The Reading Teacher* 54:146-151.

Explode The Code Books 3 and 4 Teacher's Guide and Answer Key

Explode The Code Teacher's Guides expand on the skills presented in the student books, providing teachers with various options for instruction and reinforcement. The guides address the principles of phonemic awareness, phonics, vocabulary, fluency, and comprehension as they relate to each new skill presented in the lesson. They also include suggestions for writing practice and differentiating instruction. Each lesson follows the same easy-to-use format:

Link to Prior Knowledge/Quick Review   Each new lesson begins by helping students make connections to previously learned concepts or sound–symbol relationships.

Phonological/Phonemic Awareness   This section provides instruction to help students recognize and manipulate the sounds in spoken words. Struggling learners may need this kind of support on an ongoing basis in order to improve their ability to read and spell. The oral activities in this section help students focus in on and work with the sounds of words in the lesson. The activities include discriminating and matching sounds in words, and identifying rhymes. Other activities challenge students to identify, isolate, or manipulate phonemes. Book 4 also has students identify syllables in words.

Phonics   This section helps students learn the sound–symbol relationships necessary for decoding words. Teachers introduce each skill by calling attention to sounds in familiar words. Then they teach students the letter or letters that represent that sound. Students then practice the skill, working with other words that include that phonic element.

Vocabulary   Learning new words is essential to the development of reading comprehension. This section defines unfamiliar words from the lesson. It also identifies sight words necessary for completing the exercises.

Completing Student Pages   This section directs the class to the corresponding *Explode The Code* student books. Teachers read the student book directions with the class and check for understanding of the task. They identify any unfamiliar illustrations and walk through a sample item on each page. Each student book lesson follows a predictable format; as students learn the format, they should be able to complete the pages without further assistance.

Comprehension   In order for students to fully understand what they read, they need to be able to use, discuss, define, and understand words in a variety of ways. The comprehension-building activities in this section expand students' understanding of lesson words and concepts by having them answer questions, work with synonyms and antonyms, use words in oral sentences, explain the meaning of words in context, and draw pictures. Students can then apply their word comprehension skills to a variety of texts.

Fluency   Fluent readers spend less time decoding words and give more attention to comprehending text. In this section, a variety of fluency activities help students develop skills in reading sentences and passages accurately and quickly. The rotating menu of fluency-building activities includes the following: partner reading, noting punctuation, developing or improving accuracy, reading with expression, articulation, varying pitch and volume, improving rate, and phrasing.

Writing   Writing goes hand-in-hand with phonics instruction. In this section, students are asked to incorporate words from the lesson as they copy, complete, or compose sentences. Other activities have students write paragraphs, poems, or stories.

Differentiating Instruction   The rotating menu of activities in this section provides suggestions accommodating a broad range of learning needs and styles. **ELL** tips and activities help teachers identify and accommodate potential problem areas for English-language learners. **Extra Practice** refers teachers to lessons in Books 3½ and 4½ that can be used for extra practice. **Challenge** activities are provided for students who complete the student book pages without difficulty. **Learning Styles** activities address the learning styles of kinesthetic, visual/spatial, auditory, musical, or linguistic learners. **Computer-based Reinforcement** activities direct teachers to *ETC Online,* where students can get additional practice with *Explode The Code* phonics skills in an interactive, dynamic format.

Key   Answers to the posttests for Books 3, 3½, 4, and 4½ are provided.

Explode The Code Coordinating Materials

Explode The Code **Placement Test**   The tests in this quick assessment help teachers determine student placement within the *Explode The Code* series.

Ready, Set, Go **Picture–Letter Cards**   *Ready, Set, Go* Picture Letter Cards feature initial consonants taught in Books A, B, and C. The set consists of twenty sheets, each with a picture card, a letter card, and a picture card with the letter superimposed.

Wall Chart and Activity Book   The *Explode The Code* Wall Chart is a colorful felt wall chart with letter pockets containing tangible felt objects that reinforce the key words for the twenty-six letters of the alphabet and their sounds. The Activity Book for the Wall Chart provides ideas for several activities and games to further aid in learning the names and sounds of the letters taught in Books A, B, C, and 1.

Explode The Code **Code Cards**   This set of fifty-four index cards reinforces the sound–symbol relationships taught in *Explode The Code* Books 1–3. Code Cards can be used for instruction and review.

Explode The Code for English Language Learners   This resource supplements instruction of *Explode The Code* Books 1–3 by providing specific direction for teachers of English-language learners. Reproducible student pages are included.

Explode The Code **Extra Practice Books**   *Explode The Code* Books 1½–6½ provide further practice in the skills taught in Books 1–6.

Beyond The Code   The *Beyond The Code* books provide opportunities for advanced reading of longer stories. These books incorporate skills from the *Explode The Code* books, introduce many more sight words, and emphasize reading comprehension and critical thinking.

ETC Online   *ETC Online* presents the *Explode The Code* content in an interactive and dynamic format. *ETC Online's* adaptive technology adjusts the content it delivers automatically, according to the student's performance. It has extensive feedback features for students, parents, teachers, and administrators. See www.explodethecode.com for details.

Book 3

Lesson 1
one-syllable words ending in a long vowel, including *-y*

Quick Review
Have students number 1 to 10 on a piece of paper. Ask them to listen to the following words and write the letter they hear at the beginning of each: 1. *elegant* (/e/), 2. *opera* (/o/), 3. *zero* (/z/), 4. *itch* (/i/), 5. *wedding* (/w/), 6. *victory* (/v/), 7. *asterisk* (/a/), 8. *ugly* (/u/), 9. *astronaut* (/a/), 10. *uncle* (/u/).

Phonemic Awareness
Phoneme Categorization   Have students listen to the following sets of words, and ask what sound they hear at the end of each.

he, she, me, we, be (/ē/)	I, hi (/ī/)
go, so, no, yo-yo (/ō/)	cry, fry, my, try (/ī/)

Phonics
Introduce the Skill   Write the vowels *a, e, i, o,* and *u* on the board and have the class name them. Tell students that when a letter stands alone, it says its own name. For example, the letter *i* (which is also a word) says /ī/.

Say the word *go* and write it on the board. Tell students that when a vowel is alone at the end of a word, it also says its own name, as in *go*. Display additional words that follow this rule: *he, she, me, we, be, so, no, I, hi.* Have volunteers underline the vowels and read the words.

Tell students that *y* sometimes acts as a vowel. If a little word ends in *y,* the *y* says /ī/. Write and say the word *my.* Ask students what sound *y* makes at the end of *my.* Display additional words that follow this rule. Have volunteers underline the *y* and read the words: *my, by, spy, try, fly.*

Vocabulary
Introduce New Vocabulary   If students are not familiar with lesson words or concepts, provide explanations: To **spy** means to watch someone or something secretly; a **spy** is the person who does this. A **trap** is a device that catches something, like a mousetrap. **Trap** is also an action word that means to catch or snare. A **yo-yo** is a type of toy on a string.

Introduce Sight Words   Introduce the new sight words used in the lesson: *or, is,* and *to.* Have students repeat each word, spell it aloud, and write it in the air using their fingers as a pencil. Together, think of one or two sentences using each word. Add the sight words to the Word Wall and have students add the words to their personal dictionaries.

Completing Student Pages 1–10
Read the directions with students. Identify any pictures that may be unfamiliar, such as *mow* in item 5 on page 5 and *flame* in item 7 on page 7. Together, complete a sample item on each page. Then have students complete the pages independently, providing assistance as needed.

Fluency
Word Automaticity   Have students read the words on pages 3, 5, and 7 to a partner. Challenge them to read each list multiple times, going faster and making fewer mistakes each time.

Comprehension
Extending Word Knowledge   Have students discuss the answers to the following questions to demonstrate their understanding of lesson words.

1. What might you do to an egg before you eat it? (**fry**)
2. What is the opposite of wet? (**dry**)
3. Name three things that **fly**. (bird, airplane, insect, bat, kite)
4. When you talk about a boy, you say **he**.
   When you talk about a girl, what do you say? (**she**)
5. What is the opposite of stop? (**go**)

Writing   Write on the board the following incomplete sentences. Have students copy them on paper and complete them on their own.

1. She will **cry** if . . .
2. It is fun to **fly** . . .
3. I will **try** to . . .
4. The **sky** is . . .
5. **My** dad will **dry** the . . .

Differentiating Instruction
Learning Styles (Kinesthetic)   Provide kinesthetic learners with the following letter cards: *y* (written in a different color), *tr, fl, m, cr, st, fr, sp, dr, sk.* Have students build words by adding the *y* card to each of the other cards. Have them write and say each word as they build it.

Challenge Students who complete these pages without difficulty can try writing a short poem using several rhyming words from the lesson.

Computer-based Reinforcement Give students additional practice with one-syllable words ending in a long vowel on *ETC Online*, Units 3.1.4 to 3.1.9.

Lesson 2
silent-*e* words

Materials: *Explode The Code* Code Cards (Code Cards 1–5, 36–40)

Quick Review

Display Code Cards 1–5 (vowels *a, e, i, o, u*) one at a time and have the class respond orally with the name of the letter, its short sound, the key word, and the long sound it makes when the letter is alone or at the end of a word. Remind students that in Lesson 1 they learned that a vowel says its name at the end of a little word. Tell them that now they are going to learn about other words in which a vowel says its name.

Phonemic Awareness

Phoneme Substitution Have students substitute the short vowel sound in each word with the long vowel sound.

Say *cap.* Now change the /ă/ to /ā/. What is the word? (*cape*)
Say *Tim.* Now change the /ĭ/ to /ī/. What is the word? (*time*)
Say *cod.* Now change the /ŏ/ to /ō/. What is the word? (*code*)
Say *pan.* Now change the /ă/ to /ā/. What is the word? (*pane*)
Say *bit.* Now change the /ĭ/ to /ī/. What is the word? (*bite*)

Phonics

Introduce the Skill Tell students that when you put an *e* at the end of some words, it is magic! The *e* makes the vowel before it say its name, and the *e* is silent.

Write the word *cap* on the board and have students read it. Add the letter *e* to the end of the word. Tell students that by adding the letter *e*, you have turned the word *cap* into the word *cape.*

Show Code Cards 36–40 one at a time, asking the class what each card says. Turn each card over and have the class read the two words. Model additional examples, having students read the words before and after you add the silent *e.* Then ask volunteers to come up to the board. Using the examples below, have students write the first word, read it, add the silent *e*, and read the new word: *mad/made; can/cane; Tim/time; fin/fine; rod/rode; tub/tube; cut/cute.*

Vocabulary

Introduce New Vocabulary If students are not familiar with lesson words or concepts, provide explanations: A **pine** is an evergreen tree with cones and needles. A **cane** is a hook-shaped stick that helps some people walk. **Brass** is a yellow metal; trumpets and some other instruments are made of brass. A **cube** is an object with six square sides. A **cape** is a piece of clothing that hangs over your back and shoulders.

Introduce Sight Words Introduce the new sight words used in the lesson: *do, has, you, put, his.* Have students repeat each word, spell it aloud, and write it in the air using their fingers as a pencil. Together, think of one or two sentences using each word. Add the sight words to the Word Wall and have students add the words to their personal dictionaries.

Completing Student Pages 11–19

Read the directions with students. Identify any pictures that may be unfamiliar, such as *cane* in item 1 and *made* in item 6 on page 13. Together, complete a sample item on each page. Then have students complete the pages independently, providing assistance as needed.

Fluency

Developing Accuracy Have partners take turns reading the sentences on page 18 to each other to practice reading accurately. Monitor their reading to make sure they are correctly reading every word, not skipping or substituting words.

Comprehension

Extending Word Knowledge Have students discuss the answers to the following questions to demonstrate their understanding of lesson words.

1. What do you call the place where you live? (**home**)
2. What is the opposite of the word *there*, as in "I'm not *there*, I'm right (*blank*)." (**here**)
3. What do some people use to help them walk? (**cane**)
4. How might you describe an adorable kitten or puppy? (**cute**)
5. Who might wear a **cape**? (superhero)

Writing Tell students they are going to make sentences more interesting by adding words that tell *where*. Display the following sentences and point out the subject and verb (action word) in each. Have students copy the sentences and add words that tell where the action takes place. Tell students they may also add other details to make the sentences more interesting, if they wish.

1. Smell the pine. (Smell the pine *in the air.*)
2. He made a kite.
3. I ride my bike.
4. Stand in line.
5. He will rake.

Differentiating Instruction

ELL Refer to the *Explode The Code for English Language Learners* resource for additional work with this skill.

Learning Styles (Visual) Have visual learners create word cards of silent-*e* words from the lesson. Tell them to use two different colored markers: one color for all the consonants and another for the vowels. Then have them say the word on each card, reminding them that the *e* at the end of each word is silent and the first vowel says its name.

Challenge Write a silent-*e* word on the board vertically using all capital letters. Have students use the first letter in each line to come up with words, phrases, or sentences to describe the word. For example:

Kids play with it
It will fly in the wind
Tail is part of it
Excellent toy

Computer-based Reinforcement Give students additional practice with silent-*e* words on *ETC Online*, Units 3.2.4 to 3.3.7.

Lesson 3
silent-*e* words

Materials: *Explode The Code* Code Cards (Code Cards 36–40)

Quick Review

Have students repeat the rule for silent *e*: if a word has a silent *e* at the end, the vowel says its name. Review the key words for a-e, e-e, i-e, o-e, and u-e using Code Cards 36–40.

Phonemic Awareness

Have students listen to the following sets of words. Ask them to name the two words in each set that rhyme.

like, ripe, bike (like and bike)	cake, ate, lake (cake and lake)
same, game, lake (same and game)	ride, pile, wide (ride and wide)
cute, cube, tube (cube and tube)	pole, hole, hope (pole and hole)

Phonics

Review the Skill Display the following words in a column on the board: *can, at, rob, tub, bit.* Have volunteers read each word, add an *e* to the end, and read the new words: *cane, ate, robe, tube, bite.*

Remind students of the silent-*e* rule. Then display other silent-*e* word families and have students read:

take, rake, cake, lake   game, tame, same
pile, mile, tile   home, dome, Rome

Vocabulary

Introduce New Vocabulary   If students are not familiar with lesson words or concepts, provide explanations: A **tube** is a long, thin container. A **pipe** is a **tube** through which liquids can travel.

Completing Student Pages 20–27

Read the directions with students. Identify any pictures that may be unfamiliar, such as *rake* in row 4 and *pile* in row 5 on page 20. Together, complete a sample item on each page. Then have students complete the pages independently, providing assistance as needed.

Fluency

Noting Punctuation   Write a simple question on the board using words from the lesson. Tell students to listen to your voice as you read the question. Ask them how your voice changes when you read a question. Have them practice reading aloud the questions on page 25 together with a partner. Tell them to be sure to use their voices to show when they are asking questions.

Comprehension

Extending Word Knowledge   Have students discuss the answers to the following questions to demonstrate their understanding of lesson words.

1. Name some things that come in **tubes**. (toothpaste, paints, lotion, ointment, glue)
2. A **lake** is a body of water. Name some other bodies of water. (pond, ocean, river)
3. How do you know when a piece of fruit is **ripe**? (it is not too hard or bitter, it tastes good, it is the right color)
4. Name some things you might put in a **pile**. (leaves, books, clothes, toys, papers)
5. Name some things you might **ride**. (bicycle, bus, horse, amusement park ride)

Writing   Write on the board the following incomplete sentences. Have students copy them on paper and complete them on their own.

1. I **made** a . . .
2. He will **take** me to the . . .
3. **Pete rode** the **bike** to . . .
4. She **rakes** a **pile** of . . .
5. **Taste** the **cake** and tell me . . .

Differentiating Instruction

Extra Practice   For extra practice with silent-e words, see *Explode The Code* Book 3½, Lesson 1.

Learning Styles (Auditory)   Have auditory learners name words that rhyme with *bike, ate,* and *ride.* Then have them work with a partner to make up poems or rhyming sentences using those words.

Challenge   Students who complete these pages without difficulty can create clues for lesson words and share the clues with a partner. For example: "You put ice cream on it." (*cone*)

Computer-based Reinforcement   Give students additional practice with silent-e words on *ETC Online,* Units 3.2.4 to 3.3.7.

Lesson 4
silent *e* with consonant blends

Quick Review

Ask students: "Who remembers the rule for silent *e*?" and call on someone to say it: If a word has a silent *e* at the end, the vowel says its name. Ask the class to read the following words as you write them on the board. Show how you add, substitute, or delete one letter each time to make a new word: *spin, pin, pine, fine, fin, din, dine, dime, time, tame, same, Sam.*

Phonemic Awareness

Phoneme Addition and Deletion   Tell students you are going to make new words by adding beginning sounds. Start by asking students to add /s/ to the beginning of the word *mile,* and say the new word (*smile*). Have volunteers add a beginning sound to the exercises below and say the new words:

1. Add /s/ to *Kate.* What is the word? (skate)
2. Add /p/ to *lane.* What is the word? (plane)
3. Add /s/ to *tone.* What is the word? (stone)

Then ask students to create new words by *taking away* a beginning sound:

1. What is *spine* without the /s/? (pine)
2. What is *globe* without the /g/? (lobe)
3. What is *plate* without the /p/? (late)

Phonics

Introduce the Skill   Remind students that they have already learned about initial blends and silent-*e* words. In this lesson they will be working with words that have both an initial blend and a silent *e*.

Display the following words in a column and read them with the class: *pine, lobe, late, lane, lame, tone,* and *mile.* Then display the letters *f, g, s,* and *p.* Tell students that they will be choosing a letter to add to the beginning of a word in the list to make a new word. Have volunteers come to the board, add a letter, and read the new word. Answers: *spine, globe, plate/slate, plane, flame, stone,* and *smile.*

Vocabulary

Introduce New Vocabulary   If students are not familiar with lesson words or concepts, provide explanations: A **blade** is the sharp metal part of a knife or ice skate. A **flame** is the flickering bit of fire that you might see at the tip of a candle. A **flake** can be snow crystals gathered together to form a snow**flake**.

Introduce Sight Words   Introduce the new sight word used in the lesson: *with.* Have students repeat the word, spell it aloud, and write it in the air using their fingers as a pencil. Together, think of one or two sentences using the word. Add the sight word to the Word Wall and have students add it to their personal dictionaries.

Completing Student Pages 28–35

Read the directions with students. Identify any pictures that may be unfamiliar, such as *stone* in row 2 on page 28; *plum* in item 1 and *sale* in item 2 on page 30; and *snack* in item 5 on page 32. Together, complete a sample item on each page. Then have students complete the pages independently, providing assistance as needed.

Fluency

Word Automaticity   Have students read with a partner the words from one of the pages in the lesson. Challenge them to read each list multiple times, going faster and making fewer mistakes each time.

Comprehension

Extending Word Knowledge   Have students discuss the answers to the following questions to demonstrate their understanding of lesson words.

1. You might see this coming out of a chimney. (**smoke**)
2. On what kitchen appliance do you cook a meal? (**stove**)
3. What can you fly in when you go on a trip? (**plane**)
4. What is another word for rock? (**stone**)
5. If something makes you happy, your face will probably do this. (**smile**)

Writing   Tell students they are going to make sentences more interesting by adding words that tell *when*. Display the following sentences and point out the subject and verb (action word) in each. Have students copy the sentences and add words that tell when the action takes place. Tell students they may also add other details to make the sentences more interesting, if they wish.

1. The plane lands. (The plane lands *at five*.)
2. We smile.
3. Blake ate grapes.
4. The flakes fell.
5. Dale broke the skate.

Differentiating Instruction

Extra Practice   For extra practice with silent-e words with blends, see *Explode The Code Book 3½*, Lesson 2.

Challenge   Write the following words on the board: *stone, slate, plate, smile, plane, bride,* and *flake.* Have students copy them on paper, underline the vowels in each word, and circle the smaller words within each (*tone, late, late, mile, lane, ride, lake*). Tell students that in two words on the board they should be able to find two smaller words; they should circle each in a different color (both *ton* and *tone* in *stone;* both *slat* and *late* in *slate*).

Computer-based Reinforcement   Give students additional practice with silent-e words with consonant blends on *ETC Online,* Units 3.4.1 to 3.4.7.

Lesson 5

digraph *sh*

Materials: *Explode The Code* Code Cards (Code Cards 41 and 42)

Quick Review

Write on the board the first word in each set below and have students read it. Then add one letter to each as indicated, and have students read the new words.

tub (add silent *e* to make *tube*)

lake (add *f* to the beginning to make *flake*)

lid (add *s* to the beginning to make *slid,* then add silent *e* to make *slide*)

lame (add *b* to the beginning to make *blame*)

rid (add silent *e* to make *ride,* then add *b* to the beginning to make *bride*)

tone (add *s* to the beginning to make *stone*)

plan (add silent *e* to make *plane*)

at (add silent *e* to make *ate,* add *l* to the beginning to make *late,*
     add *p* to the beginning to make *plate*)

mile (add *s* to the beginning to make *smile*)

Phonemic Awareness

Say *shell* and *ship,* emphasizing the *sh* sound. Ask students what sound is the same in both words (/sh/), and whether that sound is at the beginning or end of the words (beginning). Then say the words *brush* and *crash,* emphasizing the *sh* sound. Ask students what sound is the same in both words (/sh/), and whether that sound is at the beginning or end of the words (end).

Then say the following words and have students say whether the /sh/ is at the beginning or end of each word: *shut* (beginning), *dish* (end), *shark* (beginning), *short* (beginning), *fish* (end), *rush* (end), *share* (beginning), *trash* (end).

Phonics

Introduce the Skill   Show students a shell or a picture of a shell and ask them to name it. Display the word *shell* and underline the digraph *sh.* Tell students that *sh* says /sh/ as in *shell.*

Write the letters *sh* on the board or display Code Card 41. Have students brainstorm some other words that begin with *sh,* and write them on the board. Ask volunteers to come up to the board and underline the *sh* in each word.

Display Code Card 42. Tell students that *sh* also makes the sound they hear at the end of words like *fish.* Have students brainstorm some other words that end with *sh,* and write them on the board. Ask volunteers to come up to the board and underline the *sh* in each word.

Vocabulary

Introduce New Vocabulary   If students are not familiar with lesson words or concepts, provide explanations: **Shade** is a cool place out of the sun. A **shed** is a small house-like structure. When you **rush** somewhere you try to get there quickly. When a horse **trots** it is running slowly.

Introduce Sight Words   Introduce the new sight word used in the lesson: *I.* Have students repeat the word, spell it aloud, and write it in the air using their fingers as a pencil. Together, think of one or two sentences using the word. Add the sight word to the Word Wall and have students add it to their personal dictionaries.

Completing Student Pages 36–43

Read the directions with students. Identify any pictures that may be unfamiliar, such as *dish* in item 6 on page 36; *shut* in row 3, *shed* in row 4, and *rush* in row 5 on page 37. Together, complete a sample item on each page. Then have students complete the pages independently, providing assistance as needed.

Fluency

Developing Accuracy   Have partners take turns reading the sentences on page 42 to each other to practice reading accurately. Monitor their reading to make sure they are correctly reading every word, not skipping or substituting words.

Comprehension

Extending Word Knowledge   Tell students that some words can have two or more different meanings. Have students tell you what each word in bold means in the sentences below.

1. The lawnmower is in the **shed**. (small house-like structure)
2. My dog will **shed** some fur in the summer. (to lose or drop)

1. I **brush** my teeth twice a day. (use a toothbrush on)
2. He used a **brush** to groom the puppy. (object with a handle and bristles)

1. This **shop** sells great comic books. (store)
2. I need to **shop** for groceries tonight. (go to the store to buy things)

1. Can I **ship** the books to your house? (send/mail)
2. We boarded a large **ship** and went out to sea. (boat)

1. I need to sit in the **shade** and cool down. (cool place out of the sun)
2. Your T-shirt is a pretty **shade** of blue. (color)
3. Pull down the **shade** when it gets dark. (blinds on a window)

1. Do not **trash** the rest of your lunch—I'll eat it! (throw out)
2. The teacher helped us put our paper scraps in the **trash**. (wastebasket)

Writing   Write on the board the following incomplete sentences. Have students copy them on paper and complete them on their own.

1. **Trish** likes to **share** . . .
2. You can **shop** at a . . .
3. It is fun to **fish**, but . . .
4. Can you help me **shine** my . . . ?
5. **Rush** to the **shed** and get a . . . !

Differentiating Instruction

Extra Practice   For extra practice with *sh*, see *Explode The Code* Book 3½, Lesson 4.

ELL   The *sh* sound does not occur in Spanish or Chinese, and may be troublesome for native speakers of those languages. Provide students additional experience with this skill, as needed.

Learning Styles (Kinesthetic)   Give to kinesthetic learners cards with *sh* words from the lesson. Have students sort the words according to where the *sh* occurs in the word (beginning or end). Once students have sorted the words into two groups, have them read the words in each group aloud.

Computer-based Reinforcement   Give students additional practice with digraph *sh* on *ETC Online,* Units 3.5.2 to 3.5.7.

Lesson 6

digraphs *th, wh*

Materials: *Explode The Code* Code Cards (Code Cards 43 and 44)

Quick Review

Have students number 1 to 10 on a piece of paper. Ask them to listen to the following words and write the letter or letters they hear at the beginning of each: *shutter, asteroid, illness, shiny, umpire, shelter, echo, shovel, shoulder, opposite.*

Phonemic Awareness

Tell students they are going to listen for the *th* sound as in *thumb* at either the beginning or end of words you say. Have them indicate with thumbs up or thumbs down whether or not the following words say /th/: *thanks* (thumbs up), *footpath* (thumbs up), *slate* (thumbs down), *thirty* (thumbs up), *childish* (thumbs down), *fifth* (thumbs up), *shuttle* (thumbs down), *sharing* (thumbs down), *thickest* (thumbs up), *trash* (thumbs down), *thinking* (thumbs up), *math* (thumbs up).

Phonics

Introduce the Skill   Show students your thumb and ask them to tell you what it is. Display the word *thumb* and underline the digraph *th.* Tell students that *th* says /th/ as in *thumb.*

Write the letters *th* on the board or display Code Card 43. Have students brainstorm some other words that begin with *th.* Write them on the board and ask volunteers to underline the *th* in each. Then tell students that *th* says /th/ at the end of words like *math.* Have students brainstorm some other words that end with *th.* Write them on the board and ask volunteers to underline the *th* in each.

Show students a picture of a *whale* and ask them to name it. Display the word *whale* and underline the digraph *wh.* Tell students that *wh* says /wh/ as in *whale.* Write the letters *wh* on the board or display Code Card 44. Display some additional words that begin with *wh* (*wheel, when, whip*), then ask volunteers to underline the *wh* and read the words.

Vocabulary

Introduce New Vocabulary   If students are not familiar with lesson words or concepts, provide explanations: The word **wham** stands for the sound of something being hit hard. To **whine** is to make a long complaining sound. A **whip** is a flexible rope with a handle.

Completing Student Pages 44–51

Read the directions with students. Identify any pictures that may be unfamiliar, such as *thread* in row 2 on page 44, *thin* in row 5 on page 45, and *them* in row 1 on page 46. Together, complete a sample item on each page. Then have students complete the pages independently, providing assistance as needed.

Fluency

Repeated Reading Have students take turns rereading the sentences on page 50 with a partner. Instruct students to monitor each other for accuracy and expression.

Comprehension

Tell students that some words can have two or more different meanings. Have students tell you what each word in bold means in the sentences below.

1. The lion tamer used a **whip** to control the wild animals. (flexible rope with a handle)
2. **Whip** the cream before you add the sugar. (stir fast or beat into a froth)

1. That big truck has eighteen **wheels**. (round part of an automobile with tire)
2. They **wheeled** the raked leaves to the compost pile. (to move something with wheels)

Writing Tell students they are going to make sentences more interesting by adding words that tell *where*. Display the following sentences and point out the subject and verb (action word) in each. Have students copy the sentences and add words that tell where the action takes place. Tell students they may also add other details to make the sentences more interesting, if they wish.

1. The thin cone drips. (The thin cone drips *on my bike*.)
2. The whale swims.
3. I take a bath.
4. The dog whines.
5. I think I see white stones.

Differentiating Instruction

Extra Practice For extra practice with *wh,* see *Explode The Code* Book 3½, Lesson 6. For extra practice with *th,* see *Explode The Code* Book 3½, Lesson 7.

ELL The *th* sound does not occur in several languages. Provide students additional practice with this skill as needed.

Learning Styles (Visual) Have visual learners write *th* or *wh* in large letters in the middle of a sheet of paper. Then have them use colorful markers to fill in the rest of the paper with *th* or *wh* words from the lesson.

Computer-based Reinforcement Give students additional practice with digraphs *th* and *wh* on *ETC Online,* Units 3.6.2 to 3.6.7.

Lesson 7
digraph *ch*, trigraph *-tch*

Materials: *Explode The Code* Code Cards (Code Cards 41–44, 45 and 46)

Quick Review

Show students the digraphs on Code Cards 41–44. Have them repeat the rule for each digraph. For example: *th* says /th/ as in *thumb.*

Phonemic Awareness

Ask students to tell you whether they hear the *ch* sound at the beginning or end of each word: *chunk* (beginning), *stitch* (end), *ranch* (end), *challenge* (beginning), *inch* (end), *checker* (beginning), *cheese* (beginning), *blotch* (end), *chatter* (beginning).

Phonics

Introduce the Skill   Point to a chair and ask students to tell you what it is. Display the word *chair* and underline the digraph *ch*. Tell students that *ch* says /ch/ as in *chair.* Write the letters *ch* on the board or display Code Card 45. Have students brainstorm some other words that begin with *ch*. Write them on the board, then ask volunteers to underline the *ch* in each.

Tell students that *ch* says /ch/ at the end of words like *bunch.* Display some other words that end in *ch: inch, bench, bunch.* Ask volunteers to underline the *ch* in each word and read the word.

Show children a watch or a picture of a watch and ask them to name it. Display the word *watch* and underline the *tch*. Tell students that *tch* at the end of a word says /ch/ as in *watch*; the *t* is silent. Write the letters *tch* on the board or display Code Card 46. Display additional *-tch* words (*batch, catch*), then ask volunteers to underline the *tch* in each word and read the word.

Vocabulary

Introduce New Vocabulary   If students are not familiar with lesson words or concepts, provide explanations: A **crutch** is a long wooden or metal support used by people who have trouble walking or standing. When you **chill** something you make it really cold. When a person is cold and shivering they feel a **chill**. When something has a **chip**, a small piece has broken off it. A **patch** is a piece of material used to mend a hole or tear.

Completing Student Pages 52–59

Read the directions with students. Identify any pictures that may be unfamiliar, such as *crutch* in row 5 on page 52; *punch* in item 1, *chat* in item 3, and *rich* in row 6 on page 54.

Together, complete a sample item on each page. Then have students complete the pages independently, providing assistance as needed.

Fluency

Partner Reading   Have students take turns rereading the questions and sentences on pages 57 and 58 with a partner. Instruct students to monitor each other for accuracy and expression.

Comprehension

Extending Word Knowledge   Tell students that some words can have two or more different meanings. Have students tell you what each word in bold means in the sentences below.

1. Can you **chill** the juice in the fridge? (make cold)
2. I had a sore throat and **chill** when I caught the flu. (cold body shiver)

1. He will **catch** the butterfly, then let it go. (capture)
2. The broken lock would not **catch**. (close into a latch)

1. I drank a glass of fruit **punch**. (sweet fruit drink)
2. She **punched** a hole in the piece of paper and hung it on the wall. (made a hole with a hole punch tool)

1. The worm **inched** along the top of the box. (crept, crawled)
2. The bug is one **inch** long. (unit of measurement)

Writing   Tell students they are going to make sentences more interesting by adding words that tell *when.* Display the following sentences and point out the subject and verb (action word) in each. Have students copy the sentences and add words that tell when the action takes place. Tell students they may also add other details to make the sentences more interesting, if they wish.

1. The chick hops. (The chick hops *when it is hungry.*)
2. I chase.
3. We catch.
4. The bells chime.
5. I ate lunch.

Differentiating Instruction

Extra Practice   For extra practice with *ch* and *tch,* see *Explode The Code* Book 3½, Lesson 5.

ELL   The *ch* sound does not occur in Chinese or French, and may be troublesome for native speakers of those languages. Provide students with additional practice with this skill as needed.

Challenge   Write a *ch* or *-tch* word on the board vertically using all capital letters. Have students use the first letter in each line to make words or phrases to describe the word. For example:

Clucks a lot
Has two legs
Is at a farm
Can fly very short distances
Kind of a bird
Eats bugs and grain
Nests in a quiet place

Computer-based Reinforcement   Give students additional practice with digraph *ch* and trigraph *-tch* on *ETC Online,* Units 3.7.2 to 3.7.7.

Lesson 8
digraphs *-ng, -ck*

Materials: *Explode The Code* Code Cards (Code Cards 47 and 48)

Quick Review
Ask a volunteer to write on the board two words that start with *ch;* two words that end with *-ch,* and two words that end with *-tch.*

Phonemic Awareness
Have students say as many rhymes as they can for each key word below:

ring (sing, wing, thing, king, swing, spring, ding)
hang (gang, rang, fang, sang, clang, bang)
neck (deck, speck, check, wreck)
chick (stick, lick, tick, sick, brick, pick, quick)

Phonics
Introduce the Skill   Show children a ring or a picture of a ring and ask them to name it. Display the word *ring* and underline the *ng.* Tell students that *ng* at the end of a word says /ng/ as in *ring.* Write the letters *ng* on the board or display Code Card 47. Have students brainstorm some other words that end with *-ng.* Write them on the board, then ask volunteers to underline the *ng* in each.

Show students a picture of a duck and ask them to name it. Display the word *duck* and underline the *ck.* Tell students that *ck* at the end of a short vowel word says /k/ as in *duck.* Write the letters *-ck* on the board or display Code Card 48. Have students brainstorm some other short vowel words that end with -ck. Display some of these words, then ask volunteers to underline the ck in each.

Vocabulary

Introduce New Vocabulary   If students are not familiar with lesson words or concepts, provide explanations: A **tack** is a short nail. When a bee **stings,** it pricks you with a sharp, pointed part of its body.

Introduce Sight Words   Introduce the new sight word used in the lesson: *have.* Have students repeat the word, spell it aloud, and write it in the air using their fingers as a pencil. Together, think of one or two sentences using the word. Add the sight word to the Word Wall and have students add it to their personal dictionaries.

Completing Student Pages 60–67

Read the directions with students. Identify any pictures that may be unfamiliar, such as *thing* in row 3 on page 61, and *hang* (laundry) in item 7 on page 62. Together, complete a sample item on each page. Then have students complete the pages independently, providing assistance as needed.

Fluency

Word Automaticity   Have students read the words from one of the pages in the lesson to a partner. Challenge them to read each list multiple times, going faster and making fewer mistakes each time.

Comprehension

Extending Word Knowledge   Tell students that some words can have two or more different meanings. Have students tell you what each word in bold means in the sentences below.

1. I wear a **ring** on my index finger. (band of metal or other material worn on the finger)
2. When the bell **rings,** recess is over. (makes a ringing sound)

1. Put a **lock** on your bike when you go inside. (device that fastens something)
2. Mom **locks** the door behind her. (fasten with a lock)

1. Without tape, the decorations will not **stick** to the wall. (attach)
2. If I throw a **stick,** my dog will fetch it. (small piece of wood)

1. Let's **hang** your painting on the wall. (fasten)
2. My dog **hangs** her head when she knows she has done something wrong. (droops)

Writing   Tell students they are going to make sentences more interesting by adding words that tell *where* and *when.* Display the following sentences and point out the subject and verb (action word) in each. Have students copy the sentences and add words that tell where and when the action takes place. Tell students they may also add other details to make the sentences more interesting, if they wish.

1. I swing. (I swing *at the park after lunch.*)
2. The bell rings.
3. The duck quacks.
4. My mom brings.
5. Hang the wet hat.

Differentiating Instruction

Extra Practice   For extra practice with *-ck* and *-ng*, see *Explode The Code* Book 3½, Lesson 3.

ELL   The *ng* sound does not occur in several languages. Provide students additional experience with this skill as needed.

Learning Styles (Auditory)   Have auditory learners make lists of rhyming *-ng* or *-ck* words (*sing, thing, wing* or *stack, back, pack, Jack*), and write them on the board. Then have students provide oral sentences using at least two of the rhyming words (**Jack** ate a **stack** of *pancakes.*) Display the sentences on the board.

Computer-based Reinforcement   Give students additional practice with digraphs *-ng* and *-ck* on *ETC Online*, Units 3.8.2 to 3.8.7.

Lesson 9

Review Lesson: digraphs with silent *e*

Materials: *Explode The Code* Code Cards
(Code Cards 36–48)

Link to Prior Knowledge

Present Code Cards 36–48 one at a time and have the class respond orally with the names of the letters, their sounds, and the corresponding key words.

Phonemic Awareness

Phoneme Identity   Read the following sets of words, and have students name the two words in each set with the same ending sound. Present the first item as an example, if necessary.

sang, wrong, spin (sang and wrong; *ng* ending)
mock, sack, catch (mock and sack; *ck* ending)
math, stuck, crack (stuck and crack; *ck* ending)
hand, thing, clang (thing and clang; *ng* ending)
rack, truck, hitch (rack and truck; *ck* ending)

Then have students name the two words in each set with the same beginning sound:

chase, shape, check (chase and check; *ch* beginning)
whale, whittle, bale (whale and whittle; *wh* beginning)
thirsty, chipper, thankful (thirsty and thankful; *th* beginning)
shipping, short, chuckle (shipping and short; *sh* beginning)

Phonics

Review the Skill   Play Spelling Bingo to review words from Lessons 1–9. Give each student a piece of paper with a blank 5x5 grid (25 squares). Model drawing a star in the middle box for a free space. Then dictate words from Lessons 1–9 and have students write one word in each box wherever they like. Call out the words in random order and have students put markers on each word as it is called. The first person to yell Bingo (and have all the words in that row spelled correctly) is the winner.

Vocabulary

Introduce New Vocabulary   If students are not familiar with lesson words or concepts, provide explanations: **Ping-pong** (also called table tennis) is a sport played with small paddles and a ball on a table with a net. **Tick-tock** is the sound a clock makes. A **sketch** is a drawing; when you **sketch** something you draw it.

Introduce Sight Words   Introduce the new sight word used in the lesson: *of.* Have students repeat the word, spell it aloud, and write it in the air using their fingers as a pencil. Together, think of one or two sentences using the word. Add the sight word to the Word Wall and have students add it to their personal dictionaries.

Completing Student Pages 68–74

Read the directions with students. Identify any pictures that may be unfamiliar, such as *shake* in row 1 and *shape* in row 3 on page 68. Together, complete a sample item on each page. Then have students complete the pages independently, providing assistance as needed.

Fluency

Developing Accuracy   Have partners take turns reading the sentences on pages 72–73 to each other to practice reading accurately. Monitor their reading to make sure they are correctly reading every word, not skipping or substituting words.

Comprehension

Write the words *shake, whine, chase, scare, shine, shape,* and *froze* on individual notecards. Hold up a card and ask a volunteer to make up a sentence using the word. Continue through the words until everyone has had a turn.

Writing   Provide students with the following story starters and have them choose one to write a short story. Encourage the use of as many review words as possible.

> The dog **chased** the **snake** into a **hole** . . .
> The **lake froze**, so I got my **skates** . . .
> Mr. Wong had to chop six branches off the **pine** tree . . .
> The clock struck **five** and what did I see?

Differentiating Instruction

Extra Practice   For similar review, see *Explode The Code* Book 3½, Lesson 8.

Learning Styles (Visual/Kinesthetic)   Provide visual and kinesthetic learners with a set of cards such as the following: *w, s, c, t, sl, sh, ch, th, wh, ip, op, in, ing, ick, ine, ake.* Have students build words and write each word on a piece of paper. Share words with the class.

Computer-based Reinforcement   Give students additional practice with digraphs with silent *e* on *ETC Online,* Units 3.9.1 to 3.9.6.

Lesson 10
vowel digraphs ee, ea

Materials: *Explode The Code* Code Cards (Code Cards 49 and 50)

Quick Review

Display the following sets of words and read them with the class. Ask students to say the rule for each set.

> *he, go, me, hi, be, no, we, she, so* (A vowel says its name at the end of a little word.)
> *home, here, pine, cute, sale, cone, gate* (If a word has silent *e* at the end, the vowel says its name.)

Phonemic Awareness

Tell students to listen to the vowel sounds in the following sets of words. Ask them to name the word that does not belong. Give the following example: *meat, eat, hand* (hand).

> bet, beef, wheat (bet)
> sheet, fetch, near (fetch)
> meal, weep, rest (rest)
> deer, help, Pete (help)
> dream, ten, team (ten)

Phonics

Introduce the Skill   Remind students that they have learned that silent-*e* words like *Pete* and *here* have the long *e* sound. The letter *e* at the end of a little word like *he* also has the long *e* sound. Tell students that they will be learning about other ways to spell the sound of long *e*.

Point to your feet or show students a picture of feet, and ask them to name it. Display the word *feet* and underline the *ee*. Tell students that *ee* says /ē/ as in *feet.* Write the letters *ee* on the board or display Code Card 49. Display some other *ee* words: *tree, free, beet.* Ask volunteers to underline the *ee* in each word and read the word.

Bring in or show students a picture of a leaf and ask them to name it. Display the word *leaf* and underline the *ea*. Tell students that *ea* can say /ē/ as in *leaf.* Write the letters *ea* on the board or display Code Card 50. Display some other *ea* words: *deal, bead, flea.* Ask volunteers to underline the *ea* in each word and read the word.

Vocabulary

Introduce New Vocabulary   If students are not familiar with lesson words or concepts, provide explanations: A **jeep** is a specific kind of car. **Steam** is hot air.

Completing Student Pages 75–82

Read the directions with students. Identify any pictures that may be unfamiliar, such as *peek* in row 3 on page 75, *weed* in item 3 on page 76, and *spear* in item 5 on page 78. Together, complete a sample item on each page. Then have students complete the pages independently, providing assistance as needed.

Fluency

Noting Punctuation   Ask students how their voices should sound when they read sentences with exclamation points (excited, enthusiastic). Explain that when there is a comma in a sentence, they should pause briefly. Display an example on the board and read it. Write the following poem on paper and make copies for the class. Have students read with a partner. Those who are having difficulty should continue to practice reading the sentences with a partner until they read the sentences smoothly and show appropriate expression.

It's fun to read and read and read!
It makes me feel so fine.
It's fun to read a book and think,
"Hear me! I read each line!"

Comprehension

Extending Word Knowledge   Tell students that some words can have two or more different meanings. Have students tell you what each word in bold means in the sentences below.

1. Lick the envelope to **seal** it. (to close, fasten, stick)
2. Did you see the **seal** in the ocean? (type of sea mammal)

1. A doctor **treats** sick people to make them better. (takes care of)
2. Mom says we will get a **treat** when we finish our dinner! (little gift)

1. My sister is helping my dad **weed** the garden. (pull out weeds)
2. My uncle tells me I'm growing **like a weed**. (really fast)

Writing   Display the following sentences and have students copy them. Then have them underline the *ee* and *ea* words in each sentence.

1. Clean up the spill and sweep the rug.
2. In my dream I ate a big meal.
3. Is the leaf on the tree?
4. When the pot steams we can make tea.
5. Can you hear me when I speak?

Differentiating Instruction

Learning Styles (Visual/Kinesthetic)   Provide visual and kinesthetic learners with a set of cards such as the following: *eet, eed, eep, eap, eat, eak, sh, ch, sp, f, w, b, k.* Have students build words and write them on the board.

Challenge   Challenge students who complete this exercise without difficulty to come up with *ee/ea* homophone pairs: two words that sound the same but have different spellings and meanings. Answers may include the following: *tee/tea, read/reed, real/reel, seam/seem, steel/steal, deer/dear, feet/feat.*

Extra Practice   For extra practice with *ee*, see *Explode The Code* Book 3½, Lesson 9. For extra practice with *ea*, see *Explode The Code* Book 3½, Lesson 10.

Computer-based Reinforcement   Give students additional practice with vowel digraphs *ee* and *ea* on *ETC Online*, Units 3.10.1 to 3.10.8.

Lesson 11

vowel digraphs *ai, ay*

Materials: *Explode The Code* Code Cards (Code Cards 51 and 52)

Quick Review

Write these one-syllable words on the board and have the class read them. Show how in each case you are adding or taking away letters from the word before. Words: *me, meal, meat, mean, men, mend, send, spend, speed, sped, ped, pod, poke, spoke.*

Phonemic Awareness

Remind students that when vowels say their names they are called long vowels. Have students listen to the following list of words. Tell them to clap once when they hear the long *a* sound.

catch   rode
bake (clap)   plate (clap)
week   fetch
bail (clap)   wait (clap)
play (clap)   stay (clap)

Phonics

Introduce the Skill   Remind students that they have learned that silent-e words like *bake* and *plate* have the long *a* sound. Tell students that they will be learning about other ways to spell the sound of long *a*.

Show students a picture of an animal's tail and ask them to name it. Display the word *tail* and underline the *ai*. Tell students that *ai* says /ā/ as in *tail*. Write the letters *ai* on the board or display Code Card 51. Write on the board some other *ai* words: *train, pail, aim, frail*. Ask volunteers to underline the *ai* in each word and read the word.

Show students a picture of a bale of hay and ask them to name it. Display the word *hay* and underline the *ay*. Tell students that *ay* at the end of a word says /ā/ as in *hay*. Write the letters *ay* on the board or display Code Card 52. Display some other words that end in *ay*: *day, play, say*. Ask volunteers to underline the *ay* in each word and read the word.

Vocabulary

Introduce New Vocabulary   If students are not familiar with lesson words or concepts, provide explanations: A **trail** is a path you might follow when you walk through a forest. A **shack** is a small house that is not very sturdy.

Introduce Sight Words   Introduce the new sight words used in the lesson: *for* and *do*. Have students repeat the words, spell them aloud, and write them in the air using their fingers as a pencil. Together, think of one or two sentences using the words. Add the sight words to the Word Wall and have students add them to their personal dictionaries.

Completing Student Pages 83–90

Read the directions with students. Identify any pictures that may be unfamiliar, such as *stay* in row 3 on page 83, *pay* in row 3 on page 84, and *pay* in item 2 on page 85. Together, complete a sample item on each page. Then have students complete the pages independently, providing assistance as needed.

Fluency

Noting Punctuation   Have students read the following poem. Review what to do when they see exclamation points, quotation marks, question marks, and commas in sentences, and remind them to pay attention to punctuation marks as they read. Before they begin, make sure the students can read the sight words.

My dog and I, we like to play.
We like to run and play.
"Shall we play tag or hide and seek?"
I ask my dog Bee Jay.

Then Bee Jay runs and gets a stick
And brings it back my way.
"I wish that I could speak!" I think
He looks at me to say.

Comprehension

Tell students that some words can have two or more different meanings. Have students tell you what each word in bold means in the sentences below. Then have them make up sentences using another meaning of the words.

1. I can **train** my hamster to do tricks. (teach; also means "locomotive")
2. We are going to see my cousin act in a **play**. (theatrical performance; also means "have fun")
3. I will need to **hail** a taxicab. (call over; also means "large wet stones that fall from the sky")
4. The little lamb will **trail** Mary to school. (follow; also means "path")

Writing   Write the following sentences and have students copy them. Then have them underline the *ai* and *ay* words in each sentence.

1. The snail sat on the trail.
2. The rain made the hay wet.
3. I will sail or take the train.
4. If you stay, we can play all day!
5. Treat the stain and let it sit.

Differentiating Instruction

Extra Practice   For extra practice with *ay* words, see *Explode The Code* Book 3½, Lesson 11. For extra practice with *ai* words, see *Explode The Code* Book 3½, Lesson 12.

Learning Styles (Auditory)   Have auditory learners come up with lists of rhyming *ai* and *ay* words (*pail, tail, sail* and *pay, play, stay*), and write them on the board. Then have students provide oral sentences using at least two rhyming words (*I wish you could **stay** and **play***), and write them on the board.

Challenge   Provide students with a silent-e word and have them come up with an *ai* word that sounds the same but is spelled differently. Use these homophone pairs: *pale/pail, tale/tail, sale/sail, whale/wail, bale/bail, male/mail, pare/pair, hare/hair, stare/stair, mane/main, pane/pain, plane/plain, vane/vain, gate/gait, made/maid.*

Computer-based Reinforcement   Give students additional practice with vowel digraphs *ai* and *ay* on *ETC Online,* Units 3.11.1 to 3.11.7.

Lesson 12
vowel digraphs *oa, ow*

Materials: *Explode The Code* Code Cards (Code Cards 53 and 54)

Quick Review
For review, ask students to say what letters make the long *a* sound in each of the following words: *train* (ai), *share* (long *a*, silent *e*), *pay* (ay), *stain* (ai), *hay* (ay), *chair* (ai), *wait* (ai), *tape* (long *a*, silent *e*).

Phonemic Awareness
Ask students if the following word pairs rhyme. Remind them that words only rhyme if the vowel sound and the ending sound are the same.

goal, bowl (yes)	row, rock (no)
cot, coat (no)	go, know (yes)
glow, flow (yes)	tote, goat (yes)
flat, float (no)	pole, coal (yes)

Phonics
Introduce the Skill   Remind students that they have learned that silent-*e* words like *note* and *pole* have the long *o* sound. The letter *o* at the end of a little word like *go* also has the long *o* sound. Tell students that they will be learning about other ways to spell the sound of long *o*.

Show students a picture of a boat and ask them to name it. Write *boat* on the board and underline the *oa*. Tell students that *oa* says /ō/ as in *boat*. Write the letters *oa* on the board or display Code Card 53. Display some other *oa* words: *coat, coal, foal*. Ask volunteers to underline the *oa* in each word and read the word.

Show students a picture of snow, and ask them to name it. Write *snow* on the board and underline the *ow*. Tell students that *ow* at the end of a word says /ō/ as in *snow*. Write the letters *ow* on the board or display Code Card 54. Display some other words that end in *ow: blow, glow, row*. Ask volunteers to underline the *ow* in each word and read the word.

Vocabulary

Introduce New Vocabulary   If students are not familiar with lesson words or concepts, provide explanations: To **roast** means to bake or cook.

Completing Student Pages 91–98

Read the directions with students. Identify any pictures that may be unfamiliar, such as *float* in row 3 on page 91 and *roast* in row 1 on page 92. Together, complete a sample item on each page. Then have students complete the pages independently, providing assistance as needed.

Fluency

Developing Accuracy   Have partners take turns reading aloud the sentences on page 97 to practice reading accurately. Monitor their reading to make sure they are correctly reading every word, not skipping or substituting words.

Comprehension

Ask students to draw a picture that illustrates one of the following words: *float, throw, toast, roast, show.* Have students label their pictures with the word, and share with the rest of the class why they drew the picture the way they did.

Writing   Tell students they are going to make sentences more interesting by adding words that tell *where.* Display the following sentences and point out the subject and verb (action word) in each. Have students copy the sentences and add words that tell where the action takes place. Tell students they may also add other details to make the sentences more interesting, if they wish.

1. He floats the boat. (He floats the boat *on the lake.*)
2. Mow the grass.
3. My pet toad hops.
4. My dad throws.
5. The soap suds float.

Differentiating Instruction

Extra Practice   For extra practice with *ow* words, see *Explode The Code* Book 3½, Lesson 13. For extra practice with *oa* words, see *Explode The Code* Book 3½, Lesson 14.

Learning Styles (Kinesthetic)   Divide the room into two sides; designate the left side of the room as the *oa* side and the right side of the room as the *ow* side. Call on a student and say an *oa* or *ow* word from the lesson. Have the student repeat the word and go to the appropriate side of the room according to how the word is spelled. Have the rest of the class indicate with thumbs up or down whether they agree with each student's response.

Challenge   Remind students that homophones sound the same but are spelled differently. Ask students to come up with homophones for each of the following long *o* words: *road* (rowed, rode); *toad* (towed); *mode* (mowed)

Computer-based Reinforcement   Give students additional practice with vowel digraphs *oa* and *ow* on *ETC Online,* Units 3.12.1 to 3.12.6.

Lesson 13
Review Lesson: vowel digraphs

Quick Review

Present Code Cards 36–54 one at a time and have the class respond orally with the names of the letters, the sounds, and the key words.

Phonemic Awareness

Phoneme Deletion   Have students say the words below. Then demonstrate how they can take away the first letter of the words to make new words.

> Say *sweep*. Now say it without the /s/. (weep)
> Say *frail*. Now say it without the /f/. (rail)
> Say *reach*. Now say it without the /r/. (each)
> Say *blow*. Now say it without the /b/. (low)
> Say *steam*. Now say it without the /s/. (team)
> Say *clean*. Now say it without the /k/. (lean)
> Say *seat*. Now say it without the /s/. (eat)

Phonics

Skill Review   Display the following words on the board vertically: *me, street, teach, flake, main, stay, no, hole, toast, grow*. Have volunteers write next to each word a rhyming word with the vowel sound spelled the same way. Possible answers: *he, greet, beach, shake, rain, play, go, pole, roast, show*.

Vocabulary

Introduce New Vocabulary   If students are not familiar with lesson words or concepts, provide explanations: To **row** means to use paddles to move a boat. **Row** is also how you refer to people or things in a line (standing in a **row,** a **row** of seats in a movie theater).

Introduce Sight Words   Introduce the new sight words used in Lesson 13: *into* and *have*. Have students repeat each word, spell it aloud, and write it in the air using their fingers as a pencil. Together, think of one or two sentences using each word. Add the sight words to the Word Wall and have students add the words to their personal dictionaries.

Completing Student Pages 99–106

Read the directions with students. Identify any pictures that may be unfamiliar, such as *reach* and *braid* in row 3 on page 99, and *teach* in row 2 on page 100. Together, complete a sample item on each page. Then have students complete the pages independently, providing assistance as needed.

Fluency

Developing Accuracy   Have partners take turns reading aloud the sentences on page 105 to practice reading accurately. Monitor their reading to make sure they are correctly reading every word, not skipping or substituting words.

Comprehension

Display the following silly headlines. Have students choose a headline, write it at the top of a piece of drawing paper, and illustrate it.

Slow Goat Blocks Road
Sleepy Seal Eats Cheese
Green Paint Sprayed on Main Street
Rain and Sleet Make Road a Mess

Writing   Have students write a short story about the picture they drew in the Comprehension activity. Remind them that their stories should have a beginning, middle, and end.

Differentiating Instruction

Extra Practice   For extra practice and review of vowel digraphs, see *Explode The Code* Book 3½, Lesson 15.

Learning Styles (Musical)   As a group, rewrite the lyrics of a song that everyone knows, such as "Twinkle, Twinkle, Little Star." Try to incorporate as many skill words from Book 3 as possible.

Computer-based Reinforcement   Give students additional practice with digraph review on *ETC Online*, Units 3.13.1 to 3.13.7.

Book 3 Posttest Pages 107–110

You may wish to have students complete the pages of the posttest in more than one sitting. Read each set of directions with students. Observe as students begin working independently to be sure they understand how to complete each page. Introduce the sight words *pull, what,* and *your.*

Page 107. Give the instruction "Circle the word you hear," and dictate the words listed below. The students circle the correct word from a choice of four words.

1. spray; 2. shack; 3. roast; 4. wheel; 5. chair; 6. snail; 7. mean; 8. flow; 9. paint; 10. teach

Page 108. Students write sentences dictated by the teacher. Dictate each sentence slowly once or twice. It is often helpful for the students to repeat the sentence before they write it.

1. She will show us the way.
2. The train is on time.
3. Teach me to read.
4. Do not play in the road.
5. I sail my boat on the lake.
6. We like to sleep late.

Pages 109 and 110. Students complete these pages on their own. Simple directions are included at the top of each page.

Page 109. Students write the word that best completes each sentence.

1. treat; 2. snow; 3. cake; 4. chair; 5. tail; 6. dream

Page 110. Students read short paragraphs and select a word to complete each riddle.

1. tree; 2. teeth; 3. boat

Book 3½ Posttest Pages 121–124

You may wish to have students complete the pages of the posttest in more than one sitting. Read each set of directions with students. Observe as students begin working independently to be sure they understand how to complete each page.

Page 121. Give the instruction "Circle the word you hear," and dictate the words listed below. The students circle the correct word from a choice of four words.

1. shame; 2. crunch; 3. whoa; 4. boast; 5. choke; 6. trike; 7. speech; 8. gray; 9. bleed; 10. teach

Page 122. Students write sentences dictated by the teacher. Dictate each sentence slowly once or twice. It is often helpful for the students to repeat the sentence before they write it.

1. She can chop logs by the fire.
2. Can you grow a seed in a pot?
3. I eat toast and drink tea.

4. He will paint the gate white.
5. You get a prize in math.
6. The whale shakes my hand when we meet.

Pages 123–124. Students complete these pages on their own. Simple directions are included at the top of each page.

Page 123. Students write the word that best completes each sentence.

1. beach; 2. street; 3. wait; 4. green; 5. snow; 6. soap

Page 124. Students read short paragraphs and select a word to complete each riddle.

1. snake; 2. paint; 3. coat

Book 4

Lesson 1
Compound words

Link to Prior Knowledge

Say the words *backpack, firefighter,* and *sailboat.* Tell students that these are special kinds of words, and ask if anyone knows why. Explain that these words are called *compound words* because they're made up of two smaller words whose meanings are put together to make a word with a different meaning. Say the word *backpack* and ask volunteers to tell you the meaning of the small words, then the meaning of the compound word. Do the same for *firefighter* and *sailboat.* Tell students that this lesson is about compound words.

Phonological Awareness

Syllables Explain to students that you are going to say some words slowly in two parts. Ask volunteers to put the two parts together and tell you what the word is. Tell them to think about what each part of the word means and what the parts mean together.

birth	day
base	ball
door	knob
home	work
snow	man
star	fish
thunder	storm
wind	shield

Phonics

Introduce the Skill Tell students that they will be thinking about the smaller words that make up compound words as they read and write the words in this lesson.

Write the following words on the board: *bedtime, cupcake, seashell, skateboard, drive-way, airplane, bathrobe, haircut,* and *teammate.* Ask volunteers to circle each of the smaller words in the compound words, tell what the smaller words mean, and then tell what the compound word means.

Vocabulary

Introduce New Vocabulary   If you are not sure that students are familiar with certain lesson words or concepts, provide explanations. For example, another name for a male cat is a **tomcat**. A **wishbone** is a Y-shaped bone in most birds. A city's **skyline** is the outline of tall buildings against the sky.

Introduce Sight Words   Introduce the new sight words used in the lesson: *you, put, of, are, ball,* and *to.* Have students repeat each word, spell it aloud, and write it in the air using their fingers as a pencil. Together, think of one or two sentences using each word. Add the sight words to the Word Wall and have students add the words to their personal dictionaries.

Completing Student Pages 1–8

Identify any pictures that may be unfamiliar to students, such as *shut* in item 1 on page 4. Together, read the directions and then direct students to complete the pages independently, providing assistance as needed.

Fluency

Word Automaticity   Have students read with a partner the smaller words in the compound words they made on page 3, slowly and separately at first, and then faster as they put the two smaller words together. Have partners practice until they are reading the compound words as one word, with no pause or hesitation between the two smaller words.

Comprehension

Tell students to think of as many compound words as they can. Remind them that compound words are two little words put together. As the class thinks of the words, write them on the board. When you have collected about eight or ten compound words, ask students to select two compound words and write a sentence using them both. For example: The *sailboat* floated on the pond near the *windmill.* Ask students to share their sentences with the class. Then have students pick two other words and write a second sentence. Leave the words on the board and have the class read them later in the day.

Writing   Ask students to write five of their own sentences, each using at least one compound word.

Differentiating Instruction
Learning Styles (Kinesthetic)   Choose ten compound words from the lesson and write each word part on an index card. Have students put the cards together to make compound words. Then have them trace the letters with their fingers.

Challenge   Have students think of ten compound words and write a sentence using each.

Computer-based Reinforcement   Give students additional practice with compound words on *ETC Online,* Units 4.1.2 to 4.1.7.

Lesson 2

Common endings: *-ful, -ing, -est, -ed, -ness*

Link to Prior Knowledge

Say the words *use, run, little, rent,* and *sad.* Then say the words *useful, running, littlest, rented, sadness,* emphasizing the endings. Ask students to tell you what they notice about these words. Explain that you added endings to the first set of words to slightly change the meaning of each word. Tell students that this lesson is about adding endings to words.

Phonological Awareness

Suffixes   Say the endings *-ful, -ing, -est, -ed, -ness.* Have students repeat the endings with you as you say them again. Ask students to listen as you say several words. Have them clap their hands each time they hear a word with one of these endings.

beautiful (clap)	bathe
braid	blinded (clap)
bowling (clap)	blouse
bravest (clap)	blackness (clap)

Phonics

Introduce the Skill   Remind students that adding an ending to a word makes a new word. In this lesson, they will be reading and writing words that include the endings *-ful, -ing, -est, -ed, -ness.*

Say the word *thank* and ask a volunteer to tell you the meaning of the word. Add the ending *-ful* and ask for the meaning of the new word. Then add the ending *-ed* and again ask for the meaning of the new word. Point out that both new words are related to the base, or root word, *thank,* but that the meanings are slightly different. Do the same thing with the word *care.*

Vocabulary

Introduce New Vocabulary   If you are not sure that students are familiar with certain lesson words or concepts, provide explanations. For example, a **wilted** flower will droop down because it needs water. **Eggnog** is a drink made from eggs beaten with milk and sugar. If you go fishing, you put **bait** at the end of the hook so the fish will bite it. A **trunk** is like a suitcase, but it's bigger and holds more.

Introduce Sight Words   Introduce the new sight words used in the lesson: *was, old, her, for, come,* and *become.* Have students repeat each word, spell it aloud, and write it in the air using their fingers as a pencil. Together, think of one or two sentences using each word.

Add the sight words to the Word Wall and have students add the words to their personal dictionaries.

Completing Student Pages 9–16

Identify any pictures that may be unfamiliar to students, such as *thinking* in item 2 on page 12. Together, read the directions and then direct students to complete the pages independently, providing assistance as needed.

Fluency

Word Automaticity   Have partners read the two-syllable words on page 10, helping each other correct errors. They should switch roles and practice until they can read all the words smoothly and confidently.

Comprehension

Display the following sentences on the board or an overhead, or read them aloud. Ask students to circle (or name) the correct word.

> The bottom of the car was completely *rustness/rusted/rustful.*
> My dad and I took the boat out on the lake to go *fishness/fished/fishing.*
> Add a *cupness/cupping/cupful* of water to the batter to make it thinner.
> Mom bought me the *prettiest/prettyful/prettied* new blouse.
> His *happiest/happying/happiness* showed on the little boy's face.

Writing   Ask students to write down five song titles they know, or make them up, using words with endings *-ful, -ing, -est, -ed,* and *-ness.*

Differentiating Instruction

Extra Practice   For extra practice with *-ful, -ing, -est, -ed, -ness,* have students make their own lists of words with these endings to keep in an endings notebook.

ELL   Spanish-speaking students, in particular, may have difficulty with words ending in *-ing,* as there is no such ending in Spanish. Students who speak some Asian languages may have difficulty with the ending *-ed.* Having students write words with these endings on the board, saying them, and spelling them will provide needed practice.

Learning Styles (Kinesthetic)   Choose ten words from the lesson. On one side of a note-card, write the root word. On the other side, write the endings that can be used with that word. Ask children to flip the index cards from front to back to help them as they write the words with their endings on a piece of paper.

Computer-based Reinforcement   Give students additional practice with common endings (*-ful, -ing, -est, -ed, -ness*) on *ETC Online,* Units 4.2.2 to 4.2.7.

Lesson 3
Syllable division between double consonants

Link to Prior Knowledge

Say the words *book, time, edge,* and *face.* Tell students that these words have just one syllable. Point out that a syllable can be a whole word or a part of a word with one vowel sound. Ask students to put their hands under their chins. Tell them that each time their chin moves they are saying a syllable. Use the word *kitten* to model the skill. Ask how many syllables they heard and felt. Tell students this lesson is about two-syllable words that have two of the same middle consonants.

Phonological Awareness

Syllables   Tell students that you are going to say some words and you want them to listen to how many parts or syllables each word has. Have them put their hands under their chins to help, as they repeat each word.

cotton (two)   chair (one)
pancake (two)   father (two)
understanding (four)   keyboard (two)
seesaw (two)

Phonics

Introduce the Skill   Tell students that when two of the same consonants are between two vowels, the word is divided between the consonants. In this lesson, students will be reading and writing words that are divided between the two double middle consonants.

Write the word *batter* on the board. Ask how many word parts, or syllables, are in the word. Then ask which letter is the double consonant, and have a volunteer draw a line between the double consonants (*bat/ter*). Repeat the activity for the following words: *gallon (gal/lon), missing (mis/sing), puppet (pup/pet), narrow (nar/row), soccer (soc/cer).*

Vocabulary

Introduce New Vocabulary   If you are not sure that students are familiar with certain lesson words or concepts, provide explanations. For example, when you vote for something, you write your vote on a **ballot**. A **bonnet** is a hat tied with ribbons under the chin.

Introduce Sight Words   Introduce the new sight words used in the lesson: *from, have, do,* and *your.* Have students make up sentences using the words. Then ask the class to repeat the sight words and spell them aloud. Have them write the letters in the air using their fingers as a pencil. Add these words to the Word Wall or have students add them to their personal dictionaries.

Completing Student Pages 17–24

Identify any pictures that may be unfamiliar to students, such as *mixing* in item 5 and *raft* in item 6 on page 20. Together, read the directions and then direct students to complete the pages independently, providing assistance as needed.

Fluency

Phrasing   Tell students to think about word meanings as they read aloud. Suggest that they look for words that seem to belong together as a group of words, or phrase. Model reading the first sentence on page 23, paying particular attention to phrasing: "He is at the bottom of the flagpole." Tell students that the words "at the bottom" go together as a phrase telling *where,* and "of the flagpole" go together as a phrase telling *what.* Read the sentence aloud again, then have students "echo read" in unison. Model two or three additional sentences, then have students practice on their own.

Comprehension

Antonyms   Have students think of a word that is opposite in meaning to the double-consonant words you present. Write the words on the board. Give an example: The opposite of **sitting** is . . . (standing).

attic (basement)
bottom (top)
summer (winter)

biggest (smallest)
common (rare)
pepper (salt)

Writing   Have students write answers to the questions on page 21. Tell them to write complete sentences using language similar to the words in the questions. For example: *Can a letter be put in a mailbox? Yes, a letter can be put in a mailbox.*

Differentiating Instruction

Extra Practice   For extra practice with dividing double middle consonants, copy the words with double middle consonants from *Explode The Code* Book 4½, Lesson 1, and have students draw a line where the words should be divided.

ELL   Because some double consonants in Spanish spell unique sounds, Spanish-speaking students may have difficulty with this skill, especially with words containing *ll*, as that sound in Spanish is /y/. Provide these students with a list of *ll* words and /y/ words, and have them practice the words in order to hear the different sounds of the letters.

Learning Styles (Auditory)   Have students practice saying double consonant words from the lesson and clapping the number of word parts they hear for each word. Ask them to clap the syllables and then write the word, drawing a line between the syllables.

Computer-based Reinforcement   Give students additional practice with syllable division between double consonants on *ETC Online,* Units 4.3.2 to 4.3.7.

Lesson 4
Syllable division between different consonants

Link to Prior Knowledge

In the previous lesson, students learned about dividing words between two middle double consonants. Tell students that this lesson is about dividing words between middle consonants that are different, as in the words *problem, public,* and *picnic.*

Phonological Awareness

Syllables   Say the word *absent* slowly, pausing between each syllable. Ask students to tell you the word and how many syllables they heard. Continue with the words below. Remember to say each word slowly, pausing between each syllable so students can hear both consonants.

cartoon (car/toon)   pester (pes/ter)
center (cen/ter)   picture (pic/ture)
harbor (har/bor)   president (pres/i/dent)
thunderbolt (thun/der/bolt)   subject (sub/ject)

Phonics

Introduce the Skill   Tell students that in words where two consonants are together between two vowels, the word is usually divided between the consonants. In this lesson, students will be reading and writing words that are divided between two different consonants.

Write the word *number* on the board. Point out the consonants *m* and *b* and the vowel on either side. Circle the two vowels (*u* and *e*), then draw a line between the two consonants (*num/ber*). Now write the following words on the board and ask students to circle the two vowels and draw a line between the two consonants: *admit (ad/mit), selfish (sel/fish), rainbow (rain/bow), indent (in/dent), permit (per/mit), chapter (chap/ter), plastic (plas/tic).*

Vocabulary

Introduce New Vocabulary   If you are not sure that students are familiar with certain lesson words or concepts, provide explanations. For example, **triplets** are three siblings born at the same time. **Tinsel** is a type of decoration made from shiny strings of foil.

Introduce Sight Words   Introduce the new sight word used in the lesson: *calls.* Have students repeat the word, spell it aloud, and write it in the air using their fingers as a pencil. Together, think of one or two sentences using the word. Add the sight word to the Word Wall and have students add it to their personal dictionaries.

Completing Student Pages 25–32

Identify any pictures that may be unfamiliar to students, such as *stand* in item 1 on page 28. Together, read the directions and then direct students to complete the pages independently, providing assistance as needed.

Fluency

Noting Punctuation   Have partners take turns reading aloud the last two sentences on page 30, pausing at the commas and letting their voices fall at the end of the sentences.

Comprehension

Extending Word Knowledge   Have students discuss the answers to the following questions to demonstrate their understanding of lesson words.

1. What are some things you'd bring on a **picnic**?
   (**basket**, food, drinks, **blanket**)
2. Name some types of **contests**.
   (sporting event, chess match, board game, spelling bee)
3. When might someone wear a **costume**?
   (holiday, show, play)
4. Is your **sister** a boy?
   (no, a girl)
5. Show how you might **signal** to a pal in the classroom?
   (use your arm to wave or call over)
6. What is the opposite of a **whisper**?
   (shout, yell)
7. When you are in school, you are **present**.
   When you are not in school, what are you? (**absent**)

Writing   Ask students to write a short story about a time they had fun during a holiday or another special event. Tell them to use some two-syllable words in their stories and to be sure to write a beginning, middle, and end.

Differentiating Instruction

Extra Practice   For extra practice dividing words into syllables, have students complete the activities in *Explode The Code* Book 4½, Lesson 1.

Learning Styles (Kinesthetic)   Write several words from the lesson on individual pieces of paper, in large letters. Have students use scissors to cut the words where they should be divided into syllables. Then have students place the two pieces together and write the word on another piece of paper.

Challenge   Students who complete these pages without difficulty can try the following activity. Write ten words from the lesson on individual pieces of paper. Cut the words between the syllables and shuffle the pieces. Have students find the two syllables of the words and put them back together.

Computer-based Reinforcement　Give students additional practice with syllable division between different consonants on *ETC Online,* Units 4.4.2 to 4.4.7.

Lesson 5
Review Lesson

Cumulative Review

Remind students that they have learned what a syllable is and how to count and divide syllables. Tell them that this lesson will review the different ways words can be divided into syllables.

Phonological Awareness

Syllables　Tell students you are going to say some words and you want them to listen to how many parts, or syllables, each word has. Tell them to repeat the word and clap once for each word part they hear.

apple (clap twice)	problem (clap twice)
fruit (clap once)	handful (clap twice)
mitten (clap twice)	hospital (clap three times)
banana (clap three times)	wise (clap once)
jar (clap once)	rescue (clap twice)

Phonics

Skill Review　Ask students to name the three ways they've learned to divide words into syllables: between the two little words that make up a compound word as in *base/ball;* between a word and its ending as in *sing/ing;* and between two consonants that are the same, as in *bun/ny,* and different, as in *pic/nic.*

　　Ask students to make a chart with three columns headed *compound words, word plus ending (-ful, -ing, -est, -ed, -ness),* and *VC/CV.* Then have them write at least three words for each column. When students have finished, ask them to trade papers and check each other's words.

Vocabulary

Introduce New Vocabulary　If you are not sure that students are familiar with certain lesson words or concepts, provide explanations. For example, another word for *fantastic, wonderful, magnificent,* and all those other *excellent* words is **splendid.**

Completing Student Pages 33–39

Identify any pictures that may be unfamiliar to students, such as *puzzle* in item 1 and *chip* in item 5 on page 36. Together, read the directions and then direct students to complete the pages independently, providing assistance as needed.

Fluency

Developing Accuracy   Have partners take turns reading aloud the sentences on page 38 to practice reading accurately. Monitor their reading to make sure they are correctly reading every word, not skipping or substituting words.

Comprehension

Write several words from Lessons 1–4 on individual notecards. Have students each choose a card and say the word, spell it, and use it in a sentence. You may also wish to have students clap the number of syllables in the word and tell you where it divides.

Writing   Tell students that a haiku is a special three-line poem that has five syllables in the first line, seven syllables in the second line, and five syllables in the last line. Provide an example: *School is lots of fun./I like my teacher a lot./She* [or *He*] *is very smart.* Invite students to write a haiku using the two-syllable words they have been working with in this lesson. Students should use the book for reference, and refer back to the lists they made in the phonics activity of this lesson.

Differentiating Instruction

Extra Practice   For extra practice dividing words into syllables, have students complete the activities in *Explode The Code* Book 4½, Lesson 1.

Learning Styles (Musical)   As a group, rewrite the lyrics of a song that everyone knows, such as "Twinkle, Twinkle, Little Star." Try to incorporate as many skill words from Lessons 1–4 as possible.

ELL   Go through the book with students, focusing on the words they find most difficult. Ask volunteers to pantomime the target word and have the other students guess the word being pantomimed.

Computer-based Reinforcement   Give students additional practice with syllable division on *ETC Online,* Units 4.5.2 to 4.5.6.

Lesson 6
Open and closed syllables

Link to Prior Knowledge

In previous lessons, students learned that each part of a word is called a *syllable* and that there are a number of ways to divide words into syllables. Tell students that this lesson is about syllables that are *open* and *closed.*

Phonological Awareness

Syllables   When a syllable ends with a vowel sound, such as in the word *no,* it is an open syllable and ends in a long vowel sound. When a syllable ends with a consonant sound, as in the word *not,* it is a closed syllable, and the vowel sound is short. Ask students to listen as you say several words. Have them raise an open palm each time they hear an open syllable, and a closed fist each time they hear a closed syllable.

sip (closed)	be (open)
hi (open)	wish (closed)
am (closed)	is (closed)
if (closed)	go (open)

Phonics

Introduce the Skill   Tell students that when there is an open syllable, the vowel sound is long and says its name. When there is a closed syllable, the vowel sound is short. In this lesson, they will be reading and writing open and closed syllables.

Write the syllables *bid, re, mo, red, cat,* and *bi* on the board. Ask volunteers to write an *o* above the word if it's an open syllable, and a *c* above the word if it's a closed syllable (open: *re, mo, bi;* closed: *bid, red, cat*).

Vocabulary

Review Vocabulary   Review any of the vocabulary words from previous lessons with which students might be having difficulty. Write the word(s) on the board and read them aloud. Then have students read the words with you. Make sure they understand the meaning of the words before they begin to work on this lesson.

Completing Student Pages 40–42

Identify any directions that may be unfamiliar or confusing to students. Together, read the directions, then direct students to complete the pages independently, providing assistance as needed.

Fluency

Articulation/Accuracy   Have partners read aloud the list of words on page 41, going slowly at first and making sure to enunciate each of the sounds they hear. As students are more comfortable saying the words, ask them to say the words more quickly and naturally.

Comprehension

Ask students to choose ten words from page 41 and make a list of words that rhyme with the ones they've chosen. Point out to students that all the open syllable words on page 41 are both words and syllables that can appear in other words.

Writing   Write these words on the board: *infant, hotel, paper, tiger, monster, backpack.* Have students say each word and tell how many syllables it has. Then have them think of an adjective—a word that describes a noun—for each of the words. For example: *infant* has two syllables (in/fant) and can be described as *adorable.*

Differentiating Instruction

Extra Practice   For extra practice with open and closed syllables, have students complete the activities in *Explode The Code* Book 4½, Lesson 4.

Learning Styles (Kinesthetic/Auditory)   Ask volunteers to walk around the classroom and point to objects. Have students say the objects' names and tell whether the first syllable in each name is open or closed.

Challenge   Have students write some two-syllable words beginning with *be, tri, de, pre,* and *ro.* Share their lists with the class. Examples: *begin, tripod, decide, prepare, Roman.*

Lesson 7
Syllable division with open syllables

Link to Prior Knowledge

In the previous lesson, students learned about open syllables. Ask the class what kind of vowel appears in an open syllable (a long vowel). Tell students that this lesson is about how to divide two-syllable words when the first syllable is open.

Phonemic Awareness

Sound Isolation   Remind students that open syllables have long vowel sounds and closed syllables have short vowel sounds. Tell students you are going to say a syllable and they should demonstrate if it is open or closed: if the syllable is closed they make a closed fist, and if it is open they open their hand.

stu (open)	wag (closed)
mo (open)	stran (closed)
nect (closed)	em (closed)
mon (closed)	de (open)
tri (open)	tog (closed)
sim (closed)	ta (open)
zim (closed)	

Phonics

Introduce the Skill   Tell students that in two-syllable words with one consonant between two vowels, the word is usually divided after the first vowel and the syllable is open. Write *motel* on the board. Tell the class to notice that there is only one consonant (*t*) between the two vowels (*o, e*). Ask a volunteer to divide the word after the vowel (*mo/tel*) and say the word aloud. Point out that the first syllable is open and the vowel says its name.

Have the class brainstorm a list of open-syllable words. Write the words on chart paper, and ask volunteers to draw a line where the word divides. Hang the list in the classroom for future reference.

Vocabulary

Introduce New Vocabulary   If you are not sure that students are familiar with certain lesson words or concepts, provide explanations. For example, a **crocus** will grow in your garden in the spring, and is a delicious treat for some animals. If you **omit** something you leave it out. A **clover** is a little plant with leaves in three parts.

Completing Student Pages 43–50

Identify any pictures that may be unfamiliar to students, such as *dinner* in item 1 on page 46. Together, read the directions and then direct students to complete the pages independently, providing assistance as needed.

Fluency

Word Automaticity   Have partners read the two-syllable words on pages 43, 46, and 48, helping each other correct errors. They should switch roles and practice until they can read all the words smoothly and confidently.

Comprehension

Extending Word Knowledge   Have students discuss the answers to the following questions to demonstrate their understanding of lesson words.

1. If you **relax**, what do you do? (rest, calm down)
2. What is the opposite of **silent**? (noisy, loud)
3. In math, what is the opposite of plus? (**minus**)
4. If you **omit** a word from a sentence, what do you do? (leave it out, skip it)
5. If something needs to be fixed, what is it? (**broken**)
6. What do you call someone who flies an airplane? (**pilot**)

Writing   Ask students to choose five words from the lesson and write their own definitions for each word. Then have them write sentences using the words.

Differentiating Instruction
Extra Practice   For extra practice with dividing words with open syllables, have students complete the activities in *Explode The Code* Book 4½, Lesson 2.

ELL   ELL students whose native languages do not share common vowel sounds with English may have difficulty distinguishing between open and closed syllables. For extra practice, give students a list of lesson words and ask them to sort the words according to their long vowel sounds.

Computer-based Reinforcement   Give students additional practice with syllable division with open syllables on *ETC Online,* Units 4.7.2 to 4.7.7.

Lesson 8
Syllable division with closed syllables

Link to Prior Knowledge
Remind students that they just learned how to divide words with syllables that are open. Tell students that this lesson is about how to divide other VCV words with closed syllables.

Phonemic Awareness
Sound Isolation   Ask students what type of vowel appears in an open syllable (long vowel) and what type of vowel appears in a closed syllable (short vowel). Tell students you are going to say a syllable and they should demonstrate if it is open or closed: if the syllable is closed they make a closed fist, and if it is open they open their hand.

re (open)	shim (closed)
mand (closed)	glam (closed)
sun (closed)	en (closed)
gra (open)	tru (open)
vim (closed)	con (closed)
ze (open)	cho (open)

Phonics

Introduce the Skill   Write the word *robin* on the board and point out that there is only one consonant (*b*) between two vowels (*o, i*). Draw a line between the *b* and the *i* and tell the class that sometimes a two-syllable word divides AFTER the consonant. The first syllable is closed and the vowel in the first syllable is short. Ask a volunteer to read the word. Then have students read and divide the words *salad (sal/ad), mimic (mim/ic), finish (fin/ish),* and *lemon (lem/on).* Tell students that in this lesson, they will be working with two-syllable words that divide after the consonant.

Vocabulary

Introduce New Vocabulary   If you are not sure that students are familiar with certain lesson words or concepts, provide explanations: If you're walking at a **rapid** pace, you're moving along very quickly. Earth and Mars are both **planets**.

Introduce Sight Words   Introduce the new sight word used in the lesson: *from.* Have students repeat the word, spell it aloud, and write it in the air using their fingers as a pencil. Together, think of one or two sentences using the word. Add the sight word to the Word Wall and have students add it to their personal dictionaries.

Completing Student Pages 51–58

Identify any pictures that may be unfamiliar to students, such as *broken* in item 3 on page 54. Together, read the directions and then direct students to complete the pages independently, providing assistance as needed.

Fluency

Noting Punctuation   Have students look at the sixth sentence on page 56 and ask them what the quotation marks around *to rub with a cloth* might mean. Explain that besides using them for speech, quotation marks are used to draw the reader's attention to special words in the sentence. Then have students say what the punctuation mark is after the word *green* in the seventh sentence. Tell students that a semicolon is used to join two sentences together that could actually remain as separate sentences. Also remind students that when they see a semicolon, they should pause the same way as they do when they see a comma. Have partners practice reading aloud the last three sentences on page 56.

Comprehension

Have students discuss with a partner their answers to the questions on page 55. Tell them to explain why they answered the way they did. For example: *Will a lemon visit a wagon?* "No, a lemon will not visit a wagon because a lemon can't move on its own." "Yes, a lemon could visit a wagon in a story about magical lemons."

Writing   Have students write a short paragraph about traveling somewhere: to school, on a fieldtrip, or with their families, for example. Tell them to include where they went, how they got there, who they went with, and what they did. When they have finished, ask them to go back and circle all the two-syllable words. If they do not have any, show them some editing techniques and have them add two-syllable words where appropriate, then rewrite their stories.

Differentiating Instruction

Extra Practice   For extra practice with syllable division, have students complete the activities in *Explode The Code* Book 4½, Lesson 3.

Learning Styles (Kinesthetic)   Divide the room into two sides; designate the left side of the room as the open syllable side, and the right side of the room as the closed syllable side. Ask students to say their names and stand on the left side if the first syllable of their name is an open syllable, and on the right side if the first syllable of their name is a closed syllable. As each student answers, have the class indicate with thumbs up or down whether they agree.

ELL   Students whose native languages do not share common vowel sounds with English may have difficulty distinguishing between open and closed syllables. For extra practice, give students a list of lesson words and ask them to sort the words according to their long vowel sounds.

Computer-based Reinforcement   Give students additional practice with syllable division with closed syllables on *ETC Online,* Units 4.8.2 to 4.8.7.

Lesson 9

Syllable division with syllables ending in -*y*

Link to Prior Knowledge

In previous lessons, students learned about dividing open and closed syllables either before or after the consonant. Tell students that this lesson is about how to divide two-syllable words when they end with /ē/ spelled *y.*

Phonemic Awareness

Sound Isolation   Read the list of words below. Have students wave their hands in the air each time they hear a word that ends with the long e sound as in *bunny.*

silly (wave)	cozy (wave)
sell	fuzzy (wave)
hazy (wave)	fire
hassle	storm
castle	stormy (wave)

Phonics

Introduce the Skill   Tell students that *y* at the end of a two-syllable word says /ē/. Write *pony* and *candy* on the board. Tell students that the *y* usually "grabs" the letter before it to be its partner as a syllable. Ask where the words *pony* and *candy* should be divided (*po/ny; can/dy*). Have students read the two words aloud. Tell students that in this lesson they will be reading and writing two-syllable words that end in *y.*

Write the following words on the board: *silly, hazy, cozy, fuzzy, tiny, tinny.* Ask volunteers to draw a line where each word divides and to say the word aloud (*sil/ly; ha/zy; co/zy; fuz/zy; ti/ny; tin/ny*). Then ask volunteers to name some other two-syllable words that end with long *e* spelled *y.*

Vocabulary

Introduce New Vocabulary   If you are not sure that students are familiar with certain lesson words or concepts, provide explanations: A **timid** person is shy. If a surface is **glossy**, it's very smooth and shiny. **Ivy** is a green vine.

Introduce Sight Words   Introduce the new sight word used in the lesson: *was.* Have students repeat the word, spell it aloud, and write it in the air using their fingers as a pencil. Together, think of one or two sentences using the word. Add the sight word to the Word Wall and have students add it to their personal dictionaries.

Completing Student Pages 59–66

Identify any pictures that may be unfamiliar to students, such as *grill* in item 2 and *clam* in item 3 on page 62. Together, read the directions and then direct students to complete the pages independently, providing assistance as needed.

Fluency

Developing Accuracy   Multiple oral readings will help students read more accurately and improve their reading rate. Assign partners and have them read the following passage line by line. Then have each student read the entire passage four times to build fluency.

> I met a man. His name is Dan.
> He is a handy, dandy man.
> He bakes a cake or mends a rake,
> He mows the grass or drives a stake.
> That Dan is such a super man!

Comprehension

Have students discuss the answers to the following questions to demonstrate their understanding of lesson words.

1. Can a maple tree be **clumsy**? Why or why not?
2. Can a purple dress be **chilly**? Why or why not?
3. Can a doll be **lazy**? Why or why not?
4. Can a house be covered with **ivy**? Why or why not?
5. Can a circle be **skinny**? Why or why not?

Writing   Assign partners and have each child write his or her own sentence using *clumsy, twenty, candy,* and *chilly,* leaving a blank line where the word should be. Have students trade papers and let their partners fill in the correct words.

Differentiating Instruction

Extra Practice   For extra practice with dividing words that end in *y,* have students complete the activities in *Explode The Code* Book 4½, Lesson 9.

ELL   Because the Spanish sound for long *e* is spelled with the letter *i,* some students may have difficulty spelling words ending in the long *e* sound spelled *y.* For extra practice, write some words ending in *y* on the board, leaving off the *y* and having students fill it in as they say each word.

Challenge   Have students who complete these pages without difficulty choose eight to ten words ending in *y* from the lesson. Separate each word into syllables and mix them up, adding an additional syllable from another word (not necessarily from the lesson). Then have students try to figure out the word. For example: *ty skin fif* is *fifty; dy ly can* is *candy.*

Computer-based Reinforcement   Give students additional practice with syllable division with syllables ending in *-y* on *ETC Online,* Units 4.9.2 to 4.9.7.

Lesson 10

Syllable division with syllables ending in *-le*

Link to Prior Knowledge

Ask students what *y* says at the end of a two-syllable word (/ē/). Write the word *happy* on the board and have a volunteer show how to divide it into syllables (*hap/py*). Tell students that when a word ends in *-le* it also grabs the letter before it to make the last syllable. This lesson is about dividing two-syllable words that end in *-le.*

Phonological Awareness

Syllables   Ask students to listen to the following words. Have them tap their desks for each syllable they hear and show with their fingers the number of taps they heard.

mold (one)	bottle (two)
hide (one)	prize (one)
marble (two)	table (two)
flow (one)	tale (one)
puddle (two)	double (two)
thunderstruck (three)	

Phonics

Introduce the Skill   Write the word *little* on the board. Tell students that you divide words that end in *-le* by counting back three letters and dividing there. Demonstrate by counting and drawing a line between the syllables in *little (lit/tle)*. Have students read the word. Then repeat this process with the word *table (ta/ble)*. Point out to students how the *-le* at the end of the word grabs the consonant before it to make the last syllable. Tell students that in this lesson they will be reading and writing two-syllable words that end in *-le*.

Write the following words on the board and ask volunteers to divide the syllables by drawing a line between them: *ankle (an/kle), ladle (la/dle), single (sin/gle), handle (han/dle), bugle (bu/gle), beagle (bea/gle)*.

Vocabulary

Introduce New Vocabulary   If you are not sure that students are familiar with certain lesson words or concepts, provide explanations. For example, a metal pot with a lid that you boil things in is called a **kettle**. To **topple** means to fall down. **Vanish** means disappear. A **bugle** is a horn like a trumpet.

Introduce Sight Words   Introduce the new sight word used in the lesson: *they*. Have students repeat the word, spell it aloud, and write it in the air using their fingers as a pencil. Together, think of one or two sentences using the word. Add the sight word to the Word Wall and have students add it to their personal dictionaries.

Completing Student Pages 67–74

Identify any pictures that may be unfamiliar to students, such as *travel* in item 6 on page 70. Together, read the directions and then direct students to complete the pages independently, providing assistance as needed.

Fluency

Read with Expression   Assign partners and have them practice asking and answering the questions on page 71. Remind students to read with feeling, vary their tone and pitch, and make their voices rise at the question marks.

Comprehension

Have students think of an *-le* word that is similar in meaning to the words you present. Write the words on the board.

fight (battle)	cows (cattle)
easy (simple)	trip or fall (stumble)
wave or wrinkle (ripple)	horn (bugle)
oar (paddle)	

Writing   Have students write two sentences for each of the following words: *apple, candle, cattle, puzzle.* They can use the sentences on page 73 as a model.

Differentiating Instruction

Extra Practice   For extra practice with words ending in *-le,* have students complete the activities in *Explode The Code* Book 4½, Lesson 10.

ELL   Because Spanish and many Asian languages have no final /schwa+l/ sounds, students may have difficulty spelling the *-le* words learned in this lesson. Write some of the lesson words on the board, using different colored chalk for the letters *-le,* and have students practice saying the sound and the words.

Learning Styles (Kinesthetic)   On individual notecards, write in large letters eight words that end in *-le* and eight words that end in *-el.* Cut the words into syllables and have students reassemble the words and sort them into *-le* and *-el* piles.

Computer-based Reinforcement   Give students additional practice with syllable division with syllables ending in *-le* on *ETC Online,* Units 4.10.2 to 4.10.7.

Lesson 11
Vowel digraph syllables: *ai, ay, ea, ee, oa, ow*

Link to Prior Knowledge

Write the following vowel digraphs on the board: *ai, ay, ea, ee, oa, ow.* Remind students that they already learned the sounds for these vowel pairs in Book 3. Ask them what each vowel digraph says. Tell them that this lesson is about how to divide words with these spellings.

Phonemic Awareness

Sound Matching   Say the following words slowly one time. Then read them again, and have students clap when they hear the long-vowel word in each group.

ship, sheep, sharp (sheep)   day, done, dip (day)

snow, snap, snip (snow)   snack, snuck, sneak (sneak)

ran, run, rain (rain)   bat, boat, bit (boat)

Phonics

Introduce the Skill   Tell students that sometimes a syllable has two vowels together that make a long sound, such as the *ai* in *raisin* and the *ea* in *peacock.* In these words, the two vowels always stay together in the same syllable; they may or may not have a consonant with them. Write *raisin* and *peacock* on the board. Ask students to divide them by syllables and read the words (*rai/sin, pea/cock*).

Write the following words on the board: *traitor, delay, steering subway, fellow, painless, slowly, sweetly.* Have students underline the vowel digraphs, divide the words into syllables, and read the words. Tell students that in this lesson they will be reading and writing two-syllable words with two vowels together (*trai/tor, de/lay, steer/ing, sub/way, fel/low, pain/less, slow/ly, sweet/ly*).

Vocabulary

Introduce New Vocabulary   If you are not sure that students are familiar with certain lesson words or concepts, provide explanations. If something is **decaying**, it is breaking down or rotting. If you want everything without sharing, you're being **greedy**. A **scarecrow** is a person-like figure put in a field to keep birds away from crops.

Introduce Sight Words   Introduce the new sight word used in the lesson: *all.* Have students make up sentences using the word. Then ask the class to repeat the sight word and spell it. Have them write the letters in the air using their fingers as a pencil. Add this word to the Word Wall or have students add it to their personal dictionaries.

Completing Student Pages 75–82

Identify any pictures that may be unfamiliar to students, such as *peanut* in item 2, *needle* in item 4, and *rainbow* in item 5 on page 78. Together, read the directions and then direct students to complete the pages independently, providing assistance as needed.

Fluency

Read with Accuracy   Have students work in pairs and practice reading the sentences on page 81 to each other. After the first partner has read, the other partner should provide feedback on words that might have been skipped, substituted, or mispronounced. Have partners switch roles. Continue switching, reading, and providing feedback until both partners have improved their accuracy.

Comprehension

Write ten or more words from the lesson on individual notecards. Hold up each word and ask volunteers to make up sentences correctly using the word. Continue until everyone has had a turn.

Writing   Ask students to write three "What am I?" questions about lesson words; have them write the answers on the back of the paper. For example: *I'm an indoor game that uses a heavy ball with three holes for my fingers. What am I?* (bowling) They should switch papers and try to guess their classmates' words from their clues.

Differentiating Instruction

Extra Practice   For extra practice dividing digraph vowel syllable words, have students complete the activities in *Explode The Code* Book 4½, Lesson 11.

Learning Styles (Visual/Spatial)   Have students draw a circle in the middle of their papers. Ask them to write the word *teach* in the circle, then draw two lines coming out of the circle. Instruct them to add the endings -*er* and -*ing* to the word *teach* and write each new word on the lines. Point out that many endings can be added to words to make new words. Have students repeat the activity using the words *toast, play, sweep.*

Challenge   Give students a piece of wide-ruled graph paper. Have them choose several words from the lesson and write them in the grid as they would for a crossword puzzle. Remind them that words can go across and down, and may intersect.

Computer-based Reinforcement   Give students additional practice with vowel digraph syllables *(ai, ay, ear, ee, oa, ow)* on *ETC Online,* Units 4.11.2 to 4.11.7.

Lesson 12
Syllable division with three-syllable words

Link to Prior Knowledge

Remind students that they have learned about open and closed syllables, and when and where to divide two-syllable words. Tell students that in this lesson they will be applying what they've learned to three-syllable words.

Phonological Awareness

Syllables   Tell students you are going to say a word in syllables. Say /tur/ /key/ and ask students what the word is (*turkey*). Have them repeat /tur/ /key/ and tell you how many syllables they hear. Now say the syllables /bas/ /ket/ /ball/ and ask students what the word is (*basketball*). Have them repeat the word and tell you how many syllables they heard this time. Continue with the following words, having the class repeat the word as they tap the syllables.

donut (two)	strong (one)
rodeo (three)	banana (three)
runway (two)	decorate (three)
united (three)	lucky (two)
beginning (three)	alphabet (three)

Phonics

Introduce the Skill   Tell students that they can use the rules they already learned about dividing syllables and apply them to the three-syllable words they will be reading and writing in this lesson.

Write the following headings on the board: *two vowels together, -y, -le.* Say the following words one at a time: *remainder, unhappy, unstable, slippery.* Have a volunteer write each word in the proper column and divide it into syllables (*two vowels together: re/main/der; -y: un/hap/py; slip/pe/ry; -le: un/sta/ble*).

Vocabulary

Introduce New Vocabulary   If you are not sure that students are familiar with certain lesson words or concepts, provide explanations. For example, to **calculate** means to add, subtract, multiply, and/or divide. If you are **eager** to do something, you are excited—you can't wait! A **runway** is a road that airplanes travel on before taking off or after they land. A **telescope** is an instrument used to see things far away, like stars and planets. A **bundle** is a small package.

Completing Student Pages 83–90

Identify any pictures that may be unfamiliar to students, such as *tomato* in row 3 on page 84; *volcano* in row 1, *skip* in row 2, and *cucumber* and *ice cube* in row 5 on page 86. Together, read the directions and then direct students to complete the pages independently, providing assistance as needed.

Fluency

Varying Pitch and Volume   Have students take turns reading page 89 to a partner, practicing changing the pitch and volume of their voices as they read.

Comprehension

Extending Word Knowledge   Have students discuss the answers to the following questions to demonstrate their understanding of lesson words.

1. At what time of year might you have snow and freezing temperatures?
   (**wintertime**)
2. What animal is similar to an alligator? (**crocodile**)
3. Name the months of the year that have three syllables.
   (**September, October, November, December**)
4. What are some insects that have three syllables in their names?
   (**bumblebees, grasshoppers**)
5. Name a three-syllable word that is a synonym for *sad.*
   (**unhappy**)

Writing   Have students write a paragraph about their pet, a pet they once had, or their ideal pet, using at least five three-syllable words in their writing. Suggest that they describe what the pet looks like, tell what it eats, and tell something special about it.

Differentiating Instruction

Extra Practice   For extra practice dividing three-syllable words, have students complete the activities in *Explode The Code* Book 4½, Lesson 11.

Learning Styles (Musical)   Choose a short passage from one of the students' favorite books. Distribute instruments such as sticks, bells, tambourines, and maracas. Tell students that they will be using their instruments to tap out the syllables they hear as you read. Begin to read the words in phrases, allowing time for students to strike/blow/shake their instruments once for each syllable they hear.

Challenge   Have students who complete these pages without difficulty solve the following word equations. Tell students to choose a syllable from each word in the equation that when put together, will equal a three-syllable lesson word.

> volume + canine + notion = ? (volcano: *vol* from *vol/ume, cā* from *ca/nine,*
>   *nō* from *no/tion*)
> total + major + total = ? (tomato: *tō* from *to/tal, mā* from *ma/jor, tō* from *to/tal*)
> hostile + pity + talent = ? (hospital: *hos* from *hos/pit/al, pi* from *pi/ty, tal* from *tal/ent*)
> calendar + cucumber + lately = ? (calculate: *cal* from *cal/en/dar, cu* from *cu/cum/ber,*
>   *late* from *late/ly*)
> accept + robot + battle = ? (acrobat: *ac* from *ac/cept, ro* from *ro/bot, bat* from *bat/tle*)

Computer-based Reinforcement   Give students additional practice with syllable division with three-syllable words on *ETC Online,* Units 4.12.3 to 4.12.7.

Book 4 Posttest Pages 91–94

You may wish to have students complete the pages of the posttest in more than one sitting. Read each set of directions with students. Observe as students begin working independently to be sure they understand how to complete each page.

Page 91. Students divide words into syllables and mark the vowel in the first syllable long or short according to the directions.

bā|con	căb|in	sī|lent	ĕx|pense
rē|fuse	lā|ter	dē|mand	hŭn|gry
rŏb|in	răb|bit	chō|sen	mā|ple
fĭn|ish	sŏl|id	wĭg|gle	ē|vent
căm|pus	vĕl|vet	stā|ble	fŭn|ny
bŭn|dle	prō|tect	fāith|ful	hăb|it
cŏp|per	tăb|let	ăb|sent	fī|nal
nō|ble	bō|nus	sĭm|ple	hū|man
prŏp|er	răd|ish	rē|main	ē|lect
ăd|mit	prō|gram	nŭt|meg	jŏl|ly

Page 92. Give the instruction "Circle the word you hear," and dictate the words listed below. The students circle the correct word from a choice of five words.

1. thimble; 2. result; 3. collect; 4. shelter; 5. pretend; 6. blossom; 7. explore; 8. beneath; 9. rapidly; 10. president

Page 93. Students write sentences dictated by the teacher. Dictate each sentence slowly once or twice. It is often helpful for the students to repeat the sentence before they write it.

1. The airplane is landing on the windy runway.
2. The rubber bunny floated in the soapy bathtub.
3. In a moment the spider will swing onto the table.
4. He is eating twenty pink cupcakes rapidly.
5. The triplets win a prize in a contest.

Page 94. Students complete this page on their own. Simple directions are included at the top of the page. Students read short paragraphs and select words from a list to complete each paragraph sensibly.

1. begins, teacher, lazy, remain, windows, rabbit, papers
2. chilly, mailbox, bundle, mittens, splashing, lucky
3. baseball, shopping, basket, tomato, chicken, lemonade

Book 4½ Posttest Pages 100–104

You may wish to have students complete the pages of the posttest in more than one sitting. Read each set of directions with students. Observe as students begin working independently to be sure they understand how to complete each page.

Page 100. Give the instruction "Circle the word you hear," and dictate the words listed below. The students circle the correct word from a choice of four words.

1. sliver; 2. athlete; 3. complain; 4. bumpy; 5. credit; 6. rotate; 7. sample; 8. tropics; 9. propeller; 10. volunteer

Page 101. Students write sentences dictated by the teacher. Dictate each sentence slowly once or twice. It is often helpful for the students to repeat the sentence before they write it.

1. Tony had a tantrum when his trombone got bent.
2. When it rains on a sunny day, you may see a rainbow.
3. The reptile has a dimple when it smiles.
4. The smoky volcano may erupt.
5. My playmate is ticklish under her chin.

Page 102. Students divide words into syllables and mark the vowel in the first syllable long or short according to the directions.

rē|lax	rāil|road	tĕm|pest	hĕlp|ful
crā|zy	dĭc|tate	fĕl|low	crăck|pot
tī|tle	bē|gin	măd|ness	ĭn|fect
thĭm|ble	hăm|ster	sprĭn|kle	mī|nus
ŭg|ly	dĭs|tress	spĭn|ach	mĭs|take
chŏp|py	drīve|way	ĭn|sult	sun|rise
bā|sin	rĭd|dle	rēa|son	rĕl|ish
pŭb|lic	prŏf|it	bē|long	wēek|end
rāin|bow	hō|ly	tăn|trum	fĭn|ish
stăm|pede	fā|ble	bē|neath	hănd|ful
sŭs|pend	cŏm|ic	nŏs|tril	lō|cate

Pages 103–104. Students complete these pages on their own. Simple directions are included at the top of each page. Students read short paragraphs and select words from a list to complete each paragraph sensibly.

1. athlete, sneakers, slowly, rainy, puddle, relax
2. table, menu, pineapple, chopsticks, teapot, China
3. sea, butterfly, rowboat, stingray, appears, diver

Posttest Scores

- **80% of items correct:** Mastery of skills presented in Book 4.
- **Less than 80% of items correct:** Review skills in Book 4 as needed.